GUARDIANS

of the DREAM

GUARDIANS

of the DREAM

The Enduring Legacy of
America's Immigrants

PAUL HSU

MAXWELL PUBLISHING LLC
FORT WALTON BEACH, FL

Published by
Maxwell Publishing LLC
Fort Walton Beach, FL

Publisher's Cataloging-in-Publication Data
Hsu, Paul.

   Guardians of the dream : the enduring legacy of America's immigrants / by Paul Hsu. – Fort Walton Beach, FL : Maxwell Pub. LLC, 2014.

   p. ; cm.

   ISBN13: 978-0-9860735-0-2

   1. Immigrants--United States. 2. American Dream.
   3. Success--United States. 4. Small business--United States.
   5. Chinese--United States. I. Title.

   E184.A1 H78 2014
   304.873—dc23   2014932725

FIRST EDITION

Project coordination by Jenkins Group, Inc.
www.BookPublishing.com

Interior design by Brooke Camfield

Printed in the United States of America
 18   17   16   15   14 • 5 4 3 2 1

For my mother and my wife,
the two most influential ladies in my life.

CONTENTS

Introduction: A Patriot's View   ix

one: The American Dream: Dead or Alive?   1

two: The Enduring Power of the Immigrant Journey   13

three: Can Anyone Still Make It in America?   33

four: Individuals in Small Business:
         America's Backbone and Hope   47

five: Passing the Baton of the Dream:
         Education as the Conduit   65

six: How America Is Still the Innovation Nation   79

seven: The Secret to the Entrepreneurial Spirit   93

eight: Embracing the Gift of Diversity   109

nine: Believing in America . . .
         Who Are the Guardians?   123

Appendix A: Notes   135

Acknowledgments   157

About the Author   159

INTRODUCTION
A PATRIOT'S VIEW

"The founding fathers knew they were creating
what many now call a multicultural nation."

—Michael Barone

I am an immigrant to this great country, the United States of America. I came here from Taiwan 38 years ago to fulfill my own dream. In the process I became a shepherd of the American Dream.

This book is about my story and my vision for America's continuous greatness. The promise of "life, liberty, and the pursuit of happiness" has real meaning to immigrants like me. In every community across this nation, we can share success stories. And while many Americans have grown discouraged in the wake of economic instability and political tension, an argument should be made for optimism.

"The future belongs to those who believe in the beauty of their dreams," Eleanor Roosevelt once said. In my own tradition, there is a well-known proverb: "Better to light a candle than to curse the darkness." America has built the greatest nation on earth. The challenge for all people standing on this hallowed ground is to look inside themselves and find the will to recognize the American Dream in their own lives. This book is a road map for that journey.

Guardians of the Dream offers a hopeful narrative, based on the experiences and lessons from my own American journey and those of other immigrants who have embraced life in America. I invite those who fear that there are no opportunities left here to recommit themselves to the bright promise of this wonderful country.

In *Guardians of the Dream,* I ask some critical and timely questions to stir the American psyche:

- Is the American Dream dead or alive?

- Do we still believe in the America of immigrants?

- Can anyone make it in America today?

- How can we prepare the next generation for success?

- How can we encourage the prosperity of small businesses?

- What will it mean for us to maintain our legacy as the most innovative nation?

- What is the contribution of the entrepreneurial spirit to America?

- Can we thrive in diversity?

- What can immigrants teach all Americans?

- Can America continue to be great?

These are not easy questions to answer. We live in complicated times. In 1776, when America became a nation, there were only two and a half million people in 13 colonies. Today we are more than 300 million people spread across 50 states. The genius of divided government also produces turbulence. Although we may agree about America's principles, there is plenty of room for disagreement regarding their execution. It's not always so clear what the Founding Fathers intended, nor is it clear how to mediate the current turbulence that could not have been imagined in 1776 to create forward momentum.

In telling my personal story and those of other immigrants, *Guardians of the Dream* makes the case that immigrants are an integral part of the American texture—often called a salad bowl—and as such are overseers of a lasting legacy. At its heart, America has always been and continues to be an immigrant nation. Throughout its history, travelers have endured great hardship to come here with hope in their hearts. It is a hope that stretches across boundaries of race, religion, and class; it is the common purpose we share. What will we now make of this great opportunity?

one

THE AMERICAN DREAM: DEAD OR ALIVE?

Americans say they are fed up. Poll after poll reflect dissatisfaction, outrage, and despair. Many no longer see the United States as the greatest country in the world. Many feel like victims of forces they can't control. Many have lost faith in the adage that if they work hard and play by the rules, they'll get ahead—which is the very definition of the American Dream. People have given up on Old Glory.

Americans turn to TV or the Internet and are bombarded with negativity. The loudest voices these days are not those who are proud of our country; they are those who look around and see conflict and outrage—unemployment, unaffordable housing, inaccessible health care, wars, and a crumbling infrastructure. They are suspicious of government and have lost confidence in our institutions. The nature of news and media keeps this negative drumbeat alive.

When young people are asked about the American Dream, they are cynical. One recent survey found that 63 percent of college graduates believe that the American Dream is dead. This pessimism may be fueled by the burden of student loan debt; the weak job picture; and the continuing maelstrom of negative news, political polarization, and resulting antipathy. America's youth fear they will never have a chance to use their expensive degrees.

Many are disgruntled. If they have one, they hate their job. They complain, "I spent four years in college, and I'm waiting tables."

It's not just the youth who are disgruntled. A CBS News poll found that one in three Americans say they are "angry" with Washington. They point to stalemate, partisanship, and lack of focus on the real problems in favor of political maneuvering. These angry survey respondents look at government and find it broken—perhaps irretrievably. And they're making their voices heard: a growing number of groups have sprung up on the Web with the words "fed up" in their name.

So much negativity can be poisonous and viral. Is there any truth to this portrait? Is America on the decline? We have our problems, but when I listen to the complaints, especially from the younger generation, I sometimes feel that the real problem is not with America but in their own hearts. Many have a false sense of entitlement. They think the American Dream means they should have everything handed to them on a silver platter. They don't want to make sacrifices or start at the bottom and work their way up.

My message to young people is that possibilities remain unlimited and that it's up to them to figure out what they want to do and how hard they are willing to work. It is not up to anybody else to decide their future. If they want the American Dream, they have to create it in their own lives.

Amid this cacophony of dissent, the one group that says it still believes in America is immigrants.

I CAME TO THE UNITED STATES from Taiwan 38 years ago to find the American Dream. I was a young immigrant with a passion to succeed and $500 in my pocket. In any other country in the world, I wouldn't have stood a chance.

It may be hard to imagine if you were born in the United States, but it is astounding to be in a place where you can do almost anything: *You want to work in government? You want to work in private industry? You want to be an entrepreneur? Go for it.*

It wasn't that simple, of course. But the opportunity was there if I wanted it and was willing to work for it. I believed in the dream. I embraced the opportunity and became a citizen. My wife Maggie and I raised a family and thrived. We watch with pride as our three children continue to fulfill the promise.

When Maggie and I came to Missouri in the American heartland, we were struggling, but we were not afraid of hard work. At one point, Maggie worked at Pizza Hut to support our dream. Toward the end of her shift, late at night, I'd drive over with the kids in the car, and we'd wait in the parking lot for her to be done. Sometimes we'd see her through the window, dressed in her uniform, carrying pizzas to tables. Our children have vivid memories of sitting in the car and watching their mother working. Sometimes she would look up and see us, give a little wave, and then go back to work.

When I tell this story, people are sometimes amazed, but I explain that we embraced these sacrifices as a journey we were taking together.

Our lives were often hard, but we didn't feel put upon. We didn't think our struggle was unfair, because Maggie and I knew that it was only one step along the road. It took some time, but we succeeded. We had a belief that America had great opportunities and that if we made sacrifices and stayed motivated, we wouldn't be held back because of class or race—or because we weren't born here. That is a unique aspect of America's character.

My dream was to start something of my own, and the United States was the place to make that happen. Thirty-eight years ago in Taiwan, you had to have connections or be rich to start your own business. Here, it's not about who your parents are or where your family is from. It's about your ability to dream big and the determination to get there.

Today, after starting several companies, inventing products, and even working in government, I look back still amazed. How is it possible that someone could come to a foreign country and succeed in a business where access to high-level security clearances is required? There is no other country where an immigrant can be so embraced as an insider.

I feel deep gratitude toward our country for having been treated with so much trust and given so many opportunities. I see a remarkable country that is being misrepresented by the anger and cynicism that permeate the media. Those who have lost the sense of just how remarkable this country is should look at it anew through the eyes of an immigrant. They might see a different picture.

What is the American Dream, really? What does this country have that can't be found anywhere else in the world? My answer is simple:

- Freedom

- Ingenuity

- Integrity

- Opportunity

- Inclusion

Freedom:

Many nations around the world value freedom as a principle, but only America was founded on this as a core value. The early settlers came to the new land to escape religious persecution and restrictions based on class, wealth, and family status. The American Dream promised that you could believe what you chose, speak your mind even when your opinions were unpopular, live where you wanted, and freely elect the people who run the government.

Ingenuity:

America is the only country in the world where you can arrive with nothing and become an entrepreneur. In fact, it's encouraged. In most parts of the world, they don't care how you make your money—only whether you are rich or poor. In America, you gain respect by achieving things yourself. If you have a bright idea, you can run with it. If you invent a better way of doing something or figure out how to solve a problem, you will be successful here. Look at entrepreneurs such as Steve Jobs and Steve Wozniak, who built Apple, or Mark Zuckerberg, who created Facebook. These men came from humble roots. They had no money. But they did have big ideas and the will to make them happen.

Integrity:

If you've never lived or done business internationally, you may not fully appreciate the high level of integrity in American business. In many other countries, bribery is a daily thing, often built into the system. You walk into a government agency to apply for a license or get help, and the first rule is to slip someone cash. It's routine. It greases the wheels. Even if you go to the hospital, you have to bribe the doctor to make sure he treats your family with care. And if you don't have the money, you just have to suffer the consequences. This is the reason why we're successful here: we have infrastructure built around fair play and ethics. Our practices are based on the rule of law and common decency.

Opportunity:

Even when America is down and out, we always come back. We survive wars and terrorist attacks and depressions and recessions, and we recover and become stronger.

America is a place committed to solving problems. We have that "can-do" spirit. We learn from our mistakes. Of course, we make mistakes, as all humans do. But we learn from them and usually work things out.

American opportunity is not just about solving problems but also envisioning a better future. I believe there are two kinds of cultures in the world. One is a survival culture, based on scraping by and doing whatever it takes just to fill basic human needs. Many parts of Africa are trapped in a survival state. The second is an opportunity culture. It's always looking ahead, thinking about how to improve the quality of life of our loved ones and society. That's the American way.

Inclusion:

Gallup reports that 150 million people—one in 30 of the world population—would like to leave their countries permanently and move to the United States. They cite freedom, opportunity, and the potential for achieving prosperity. But there is another reason as well. In spite of all the controversy surrounding immigration policies, America remains the most welcoming place for immigrants. Gallup found that 81 percent of all Americans say their communities are good places for immigrants. You simply do not find that inclusive attitude in other countries. In most European countries, for example, the culture is unfriendly to immigrants. It is very difficult to procure work papers and virtually impossible to attain citizenship. Our communities adapt to other cultures. We embrace them and make them our own.

This spirit of cooperation and trust infuses everything. If you do business in some other countries, often the people sitting in the room together don't trust each other. They're always thinking about how they can undermine the other to gain an advantage. Most Americans, on the other hand, have a sincere desire to reach across differences and work together. It's in our DNA.

These five values—freedom, ingenuity, integrity, opportunity, and inclusion—are the reason one in 30 people in the world today wants to come to America.

IF YOU ARE AMONG THOSE who say that the American Dream is dead, my message to you is this: Wake up. Look around. Don't get left behind. You control your own destiny. And we all control this nation's future.

If you were born in the United States and you have a negative attitude about this nation, maybe the problem is inside you. Maybe you've taken too much for granted.

We can all learn from immigrants. Ask yourself: if this is such a lousy place, why do people from all over the world long to come here?

We all know the stories of the great waves of immigration that built America in the past century; they have been the backbone of our history. One hundred years ago, immigrants flooded into the United States. They spread out across the country to the farms and industrial centers of the Midwest, to the pioneering towns of the West, and to the financial centers of the East, and they put down roots wherever they landed. My own people, the Chinese, built America's railroads, opening up the vast promise of the nation for travel, growth, and prosperity.

When we look back and ask, "Who were the greatest Americans?" it's no surprise that many of them were immigrants: people such as Albert Einstein, perhaps the most brilliant scientific mind of the twentieth century, who fled the rise of Nazism by emigrating from Germany to America; people such as Alexander Graham Bell, the prolific inventor, who emigrated from Scotland; the industrialist Andrew Carnegie (Scotland); the ballet dancer George Balanchine (Russia); Supreme Court Justice Felix Frankfurter (Austria)—the list goes on. Even Alexander Hamilton, the Founding Father who shaped America's economic philosophy, was an immigrant—from the West Indies.

What many people do not fully appreciate is that today's immigrants are currently repeating this legacy. When I built aerospace and military technology companies, I didn't realize that I was part of a vital formula for national development. But I know it now.

Look around. Some of this country's most innovative, thriving enterprises have immigrant founders. According to *Forbes*, 40 percent of the nation's top companies were founded by immigrants or their children—a trend reaching back to the 1800s. The pattern continues to this day. Our young people who have lost faith in the American Dream should put themselves in the shoes of some of these immigrants. As Patrick Lo, the Chinese-born founder of the technology company NetGear, said, "If I had stayed in Hong Kong, I would have ended up fixing radios. It was America's culture that encouraged me to be ambitious."

David Ho, born in Taiwan, is one of America's greatest medical scientists, who discovered the groundbreaking AIDS "cocktail" that has changed the deadly diagnosis for so many. Ho's family sacrificed much to come to America. His father came on his own when Ho was only five years old, and the family was not reunited until he was 12. But his parents believed that whatever they sacrificed would be more than compensated for by the future they were assuring their offspring. Looking back, Ho remembers being teased unmercifully by his classmates because his English was poor. But look at him now.

Sergey Brin, the Russian-born cofounder of Google, whose family fled persecution in the 1970s to make their home in the United States, still believes in this country. He was raised on the stories of the hardship and discrimination his family suffered. His father dreamed of being an astronomer but could not get accepted into graduate school in Russia because he was Jewish. Brin feels he has been very lucky, and he has a burning desire to give back. "Obviously, everyone wants to be successful," he said, "but I want to be looked back on as being very innovative, very trusted and ethical, and ultimately making a big difference in the world."

Other immigrants share this spirit of innovation and generosity. My big questions were always, What could I do for this great country? How could I help my community and be a mentor in business? We immigrants don't take opportunity for granted. We are grateful, and we reach out our hands to lift others up.

Today, many people are told that immigrants are sapping our prosperity. Even though the nation was founded on openness, they are suddenly suspicious of outsiders. They view immigrants as takers, not makers. This is a damning and unfair stereotype.

But the facts paint a different picture. They suggest that rather than being a drain on the economy, immigrants continue to be the source of prosperity and hope. Consider this:

- The Small Business Administration reports that immigrants are 30 percent more likely to start a business in the United States than nonimmigrants.

- Immigrants have founded many of America's high-value, signature companies, including Intel, Sun Microsystems, Google, and eBay. In fact, 18 percent of Fortune 500 companies have at least one immigrant founder. According to the Partnership for a New American Economy, 75 percent of the companies funded by American venture capital have at least one foreign-born founding member.

- Immigrants are on the leading edge of technology that is always at the heart of prosperity and global leadership. Sixty percent of all foreign-born graduate students in the United States are involved in obtaining degrees in the science and engineering fields. More than 35 percent of engineers and 30 percent of computer scientists in America are immigrants.

- Immigrants support the economy with enormous purchasing power. According to the Immigration Policy Center, Asian and Latino populations, many of whom are immigrants, spend $2 trillion on consumer goods.

The list goes on. What we see is a portrait of vitality, innovation, and the kind of business growth that spurs economic well-being in our communities.

Why do people leave their home countries and come here?

It isn't because they are cynical.

It isn't because they are lazy.

It isn't because they want to sit around and take public assistance.

No, they come because they want to raise their children in a country that places no limits on their future. They come because they want to do something meaningful with their lives. They come because they believe in the dream.

Recently, I was having a cup of coffee with my daughter Jessica. She was rushing to get to her business and could spare only a few minutes.

"Why do you work so hard?" I asked her. Maybe I was a little bit annoyed because I wanted to spend more time with her.

She gave me a look that said it should have been obvious and replied, "Because I want to be like you."

I was gratified, as any father would be. But I also recognized a deeper truth. My children believe in the American Dream because they have experienced it every day. They are American born, but they see the past and the future through the eyes of parents who found prosperity, fulfillment, and happiness in this great land.

So in answer to the question whether the American Dream is alive or dead, I can say it is alive in me. It is alive in my children. It is alive in those—native born or immigrant—who care about America and who are pioneering new technologies or medical breakthroughs or "green" designs or aerospace systems. It is alive in those who are solving problems in government or corporations, starting small businesses, and developing effective community service programs. It is alive in those who are inventing new products that will change the world and improve life on the planet. It is alive in those who feel the spark, who choose to work hard and make a success of their lives. It is alive in those who accept the premise that America is the greatest nation in the world, built on a foundation of diversity. And our best years may still be ahead of us.

two

THE ENDURING POWER OF THE IMMIGRANT JOURNEY

No matter where you live in the world, there is always America. It is not just an abstraction or a place you want to visit one day. For millions of people throughout its history, America has been a land of opportunity—a New World where you can belong, stake a claim, become a citizen, start a business, and raise a family.

President Ronald Reagan once shared a letter he'd received from a constituent that had special resonance. Reagan said, "He wrote that you can go to live in France, but you can't become a Frenchman. You can go to live in Germany or Italy, but you can't become a German, an Italian. He went through Turkey, Greece, Japan, and other countries. But he said anyone, from any corner of the world, can come to live in the United States and become an American."

This is true because, from its origins, America was created as an immigrant nation. Its vast, empty vistas cried out for an infusion of human labor and spirit. Actually, in the early periods, people didn't refer to themselves as immigrants. They were travelers, pilgrims, settlers. They came to make something that didn't yet exist. Often they were fleeing religious persecution and despotic political systems. But they found much more than security; they found an unspoiled landscape upon which they could realize their dreams.

By the time the Statue of Liberty, with its promise of a "Golden Door," was installed in 1886, immigrants had already been flocking to America for centuries, seeking not just opportunity but also equality. The egalitarian character of America was in sharp contrast to the aristocratic nature of the Old World. As Michel-Guillaume-Jean de Crévecoeur wrote so eloquently in *Letters from an American Farmer*, published in 1782:

> Here are no aristocratical families, no courts, no kings, no bishops, no ecclesiastical dominion, no invisible power giving to a few a very visible one; no great manufacturers employing thousands, no great refinements of luxury. The rich and the poor are not so far removed from each other as they are in Europe. Some few towns excepted, we are all tillers of the earth, from Nova Scotia to West Florida. We are a people of cultivators, scattered over an immense territory, communicating with each other by means of good roads and navigable rivers, united by the silken bands of mild government, all respecting the laws, without dreading their power, because they are equitable. We are all animated with the spirit of an industry which is unfettered and unrestrained, because each person works for himself.

Before the eighteenth century, the migration was primarily English, so a comfortable familiarity was built between the new and old traditions. With the birth of the United States of America in 1776, an expansionist era emerged. There was a drive west, and the faces of immigrants were more diverse—Germans, Irish, Italians, and other "foreigners."

Among the Founding Fathers, this diversity was actually seen as an advantage. James Madison believed that pluralism was a key to the freedom promised in the Constitution. "This freedom," he said, "arises from that multiplicity of sects which pervades America. For where there is such a variety of sects, there cannot be a majority of any one sect to oppress and persecute the rest." Thomas Jefferson agreed; he was openly pro-immigration, stating, "The present desire of America is to produce rapid population by as great importations of foreigners as possible." There was a near consensus on the idea that the great immigrant influx was a benefit to the emerging land.

However, with new cultural influx and diversity came turbulence. Part of the reason was economic. It stands to reason that immigrants who had gained a foothold in one generation might feel threatened by new waves. But there was also ethnic strife. There was always a question of what it meant to be a "real" American, and there was a bias toward Anglo-Western people who looked, behaved, and worshipped like the majority.

Early America had already expressed a racist bent, with both the treatment of Native Americans and the acceptance of slavery. There were even slaveholders among the Founding Fathers—Thomas Jefferson being the most notable example. How would this fledgling nation treat non-Western immigrants? I was particularly interested in the story of my Asian forefathers.

The California Gold Rush brought the first waves of Chinese to America in 1849. In the coming decades, their numbers reached more than 300,000. They succeeded in large part because of their tremendous work ethic. A poem by Xu from Xiangshan survived the era. He encouraged Chinese migrants, speaking of joy and opportunity:

Just talk about going to the land of the Flowery Flag and
my countenance fills with happiness . . .

Do not forget this day when you land ashore. Push
yourself ahead and do not be lazy or idle.

It is well known today that the early Chinese immigrants were
significantly responsible for building the first transcontinental railroad.
They were initially recruited because of a shortage of European workers but
soon proved themselves to be remarkably industrious. Charles Crocker,
the railroad's contractor said, "Wherever we put them, we found them
good, and they worked themselves into our favor to such an extent that if
we found we were in a hurry for a job of work, it was better to put Chinese
on at once."

So, in many ways, the Chinese were successful, but they were also held
in suspicion. The combination of their economic ambitions and their cultural and ethic "foreignness" led to a backlash. Increasingly, the Chinese
were viewed as aliens. Their loyalty was held in question, partly because of
their unfamiliar ways and partly because they sent so much of their earnings back to China. The anti-Chinese movement gathered momentum, and
the question of whether to exclude Chinese immigrants was hotly debated
in Congress.

The most fervent anti-Chinese official was Maine Senator James G.
Blaine. His passionate oratory against the Chinese hit a national chord
and elevated the issue beyond a regional dustup. "The question lies in my
mind thus: either the Anglo-Saxon race will possess the Pacific slope or
the Mongolians will possess it," he cried out on the Senate floor. "We have
this day to choose . . . whether our legislation shall be in the interest of the
American free laborer or for the servile laborer from China . . . You cannot
work a man who must have beef and bread, and would prefer beer, alongside
of a man who can live on rice. It cannot be done."

Blaine was the first national leader to call for the dismissal of Chinese labor, and with his fiery rhetoric, the movement gathered momentum. In a letter to the *New York Tribune* a week after his speech on the senate floor, he resorted to name-calling, labeling Chinese immigrants as "vicious . . . odious . . . abominable . . . revolting." He compared them to a virulent disease: "If as a nation we have the right to keep out infectious diseases, if we have the right to exclude the criminal classes from coming to us, we surely have the right to exclude that immigration which reeks with impurity and which cannot come to us without plenteously sowing the seeds of moral and physical disease, destitution, and death."

Blaine's anti-Chinese drumbeat had an effect, gaining support among his Congressional colleagues. His scare tactics worked. There seemed to be little interest in including the Chinese in the dictate that "all men are created equal." They were made to seem less than human.

In 1882, Congress passed the first law banning a targeted population of immigrants. The Chinese Exclusion Act suspended the immigration of all Chinese workers to the United States for 10 years and barred Chinese immigrants from becoming U.S. citizens. The law was renewed for another 10 years in 1892 and again in 1902 with no ending date.

Explaining the anti-Chinese fever, Erika Lee wrote in *At America's Gates: Chinese Immigration during the Exclusion Era 1882–1943*: "Closing America's gates to various 'alien invasions' was additionally instrumental in articulating a definition of American national identity and belonging at the turn of the twentieth century. Americans learned to define 'Americanness' by excluding and containing foreign-ness. Through the admission and exclusion of foreigners, the United States both asserted its sovereignty and reinforced its identity as a nation."

The Chinese Exclusion Act would remain in place until 1943. With China an ally in World War II, Senator Warren G. Magnuson of Washington State proposed legislation to repeal the act. The legislation, which passed and was signed into law, also permitted Chinese nationals already residing in the country to become naturalized citizens.

It wasn't the end of Asian exclusion, however. During World War II, Japanese Americans became the only ethnic group to be imprisoned en masse based solely on race. While many thought it was reasonable to question their loyalty, it is notable that no such assumption led to the mass incarceration of German Americans. The bias was selectively directed at Asians.

The Taiwanese didn't really start immigrating in large numbers until after Word War II. From the start, they were much different from their Chinese predecessors. They were better educated and less inclined to be laborers. They were seeking a level of prosperity and independence that had not been seen before.

As Franklin Ng wrote in his book *The Taiwanese Americans*, this group "helped to alter the U.S. cultural landscape." The new population brought education, an entrepreneurial attitude, and investments to the United States. They were the first true entrepreneurial immigrants—a status they maintain to this day. They were on the front lines of a progressive Asian influx. Even the most extreme nativists rarely advocate limiting Asians. It is widely accepted that Asians are America's most successful immigrants. According to a 2012 Pew Research Center report, Asian Americans (at 18.2 million strong) are the highest-income, best-educated, and fastest-growing racial group in the United States. They are more satisfied than the general public with their lives, their finances, and the direction of the country, and they place more value than other Americans do on marriage, parenthood, hard work, and career success:

> The immigration wave from Asia has occurred at a time when the largest sending countries have experienced dramatic gains in their standards of living. But few Asian

immigrants are looking over their shoulders with regret. Just 12% say that if they had to do it all over again, they would remain in their country of origin. And by lopsided margins, Asian Americans say the U.S. is preferable to their country of origin in such realms as providing economic opportunity, political and religious freedoms, and good conditions for raising children. Respondents rated their country of origin as being superior on just one of seven measures tested in the survey—strength of family ties.

Today, according to the Pew Research Center, Asians have surpassed Hispanics as the largest wave of new immigrants to the United States, pushing the population of Asian descent to a record 18.2 million and helping to make Asians the fastest-growing immigrant group in the country.

GROWING UP IN TAIWAN, I was always aware of the American promise, long before I decided to make it my own path. We all knew people—family and friends—who had immigrated to the United States to study, work, and live. The world was becoming a more open place. I appreciate how different my experience has been from that of the immigrants who paved my way. Sure, it is a risk for any person to leave his or her homeland and make a life across the span of an ocean, especially without money and with a language barrier. But for those of us who immigrated in the 1970s and later, the ease of air travel and the existence of stable families back home gave us a giant safety net if things didn't work out.

I was raised in a middle-class family, the youngest of four children—three boys and a girl. My father owned a tea company, but he struggled both financially and emotionally. He never recovered from experiencing the turmoil of the Japanese Occupation, nor did he fully embrace the new government in Taiwan. As a result, his business didn't achieve real success. There was always a dark cloud hanging over his head. There was no government helping hand, and he really struggled.

Because of my father's difficulties, my mother became a very strong woman. She was the center of the family, the one who made everything work, the one who gave us guidance and security. My mother always did what was necessary. When the family needed more income, she bought a sewing machine and learned how to sew. Then she started a business and made clothes. I still remember the children coming to our house to be measured for school uniforms. She worked so hard. At night, she spread the fabric over a big table in the living room to cut and sew. I fell asleep to the sound of her pumping the pedal of her sewing machine. When she was finished, she soaked her swollen feet in pans of hot water.

I believe that my mother made me who I am today. She helped me see a path as a young man that I was blind to because of my restless, obstinate spirit. I hated school as a boy. I hated being told what to do. I always wanted to fight authority, asking, "Why should I?" to every rule. I was always in trouble at school.

On one occasion, when I was in junior high, I almost got kicked out of school for chewing gum. When the teacher angrily ordered me to get rid of it, I spit out the gum and hit her in the face. That was a bad moment. The school was threatening to suspend me, and they called my mother. When she arrived, I was standing there with a defiant look on my face, and the principal was angry. "Take him away," he ordered my mother. "He's so bad we don't want him here."

My mother calmly took my hand and led me out of the school. As we walked along, she didn't shout at me, and she didn't threaten me. Her silence made me nervous. I thought, "Uh, oh, I'm really in trouble now." But as we walked, she finally spoke. "This school may not be a good fit for you," she said. "Let's find a better school."

No punishment. Just wisdom. She honestly believed in me. She never pushed me or forced her expectations on me. It was typical for struggling families to be almost authoritarian and prescriptive with their children. Also, my siblings were all perfect students. But my mother was unique; she never compared me to them. Her advice was inspirational: "Always be able to look at yourself in the mirror without any kind of regret," and "Just be yourself."

It would be many years before my mother's faith in me bore any fruit. I continued to be a poor student throughout my junior high and high school years. I think part of my problem was the choking rigidity of the Taiwanese educational system, which discouraged creativity and independence. It wasn't geared toward success. My natural curiosity was stifled by a system of rote learning and an emphasis on tests. It was a grueling system. Two-thirds of the young people taking college exams couldn't get in. If you were even lucky enough to get into college, you weren't necessarily allowed to pursue your preferred course of study. I spent my college years studying drama—not the field I would have chosen, nor one in which I was particularly adept. I had dreams of running a factory, but they seemed increasingly distant. Without resources or contacts, my career future was already prescribed. In Taiwan, if you didn't personally know someone who worked there, it was almost impossible to get a job in a corporation. So I was always struggling to rise above the pack and find my way, but I worried about my prospects.

My personal life was somewhat better. One day, a classmate invited me to a picnic. I noticed a lovely young girl to the side, and when I found out she was my classmate's sister, I asked whether it would be OK if I took her to a movie. Maggie and I just clicked. She was beautiful on the inside as well as on the outside. But I worried that she might be too good for me. Maggie was from a very distinguished family, and I didn't have much to offer. Could a woman like that really imagine a life with a guy like me?

Maggie had an extremely important uncle who visited Taipei only every couple of years. He was scheduled for a visit, and the whole family was getting together. Maggie told me I needed to be there. I was nervous for good reason. The night we gathered at Maggie's parents' house, it was pouring rain, and my means of transportation was a motorcycle, so I arrived a little damp. Maggie stayed close by my side and introduced me to everyone. I was polite and very respectful.

Maggie's uncle wanted to go out to a very fine restaurant, and since it was raining, we would be taking cars. Maggie's mother said, "Paul, you have your own transportation, right?"

"Yes, ma'am, I have my own transportation." I was thinking about how drenched I'd be by the time I got to the restaurant.

She turned to Maggie. "You ride with us," she said.

"No," Maggie said, "I'm going with Paul."

She followed me out to my motorcycle, and I gave her my raincoat to wear. We drove away, with her arms around me. My face was wet. I wasn't sure whether it was rain or tears. Her devotion moved me so much. I decided then that I wanted her to be my wife.

Marriage was several years away, though. In our culture, you didn't get married until you were ready to put down roots, and that was in the future. We never doubted our love during all the years and separations of our courtship.

At age 21, after graduating from college I joined the military and passed the test to attend officer training school. This was the first opportunity I'd ever had to be a leader. After training, I was sent as an officer from Taiwan to Kinmen, a small island, where I was in charge of 45 soldiers. The threat from the Chinese mainland was ever present for us, but most of the battle took place in the realm of propaganda. We did propaganda bombings back and forth. This leaflet bombing had been going on for two decades, and we "bombed" the mainland with more than one billion leaflets every year during the 1970s.

The technology was to use balloons set to drift deep into the Chinese countryside, with fliers and photographs showing the prosperity and promise of Taiwan and encouraging defection. Sometimes, food and supplies were attached. For its part, mainland China bombed us right back, with leaflets extolling Chairman Mao. We were each fighting for the hearts and minds of the Chinese people. Incidentally, many of these propaganda leaflets and posters were later displayed in galleries and museums as works of fine art.

I left the army after two years, more mature and determined to make my own way in the world. When I was accepted as a graduate student in engineering in Missouri, Maggie and I knew that going to America was what we wanted. We decided that I would go ahead and begin my studies, and then we'd get married and she'd join me the following year.

WHEN I FIRST CAME to America as a graduate student, I landed in the heartland. I was studying for a master's in industrial management and systems engineering at the University of Central Missouri, located in Warrensburg, about 50 miles southeast of Kansas City. I didn't know a soul, and I didn't have a penny to spare. I knew I was in for a tough time, but I was committed to getting a good education and being part of my new country. I just didn't know what to expect.

I had positive ideas about the United States and believed in the American dream, but it was abstract to me. Could I really make it? What would it take to survive? How could I make friends and become part of this place? All of those thoughts filled my mind. I was never discouraged, but I was prepared for hardship, especially since I spoke very little English.

But I was happy to be in a place where I could study engineering. Now my childhood dream of being a plant manager didn't seem so far away.

I was lucky to get a good advisor, who was also the dean. He advised only two or three students a year. I think one reason he picked me was that on the first day of school when I walked into his office, I bowed to him. That definitely set me apart from the American kids. To my surprise, I found that people *wanted* to help me—which was a new experience. Looking back, it is touching to think about all those who have helped me along the way, from mentors to strangers. This was my first and lasting lesson about Americans: they are the most generous and helpful people in the world.

I studied hard, but I was always worried about money. One Sunday afternoon, I wandered into a mom-and-pop hamburger place near the campus. I was hungry, and I started counting the coins in my pocket to see what I could afford. I figured out that I could just barely manage to get a hamburger, so I went up to the counter and ordered it. The man behind the counter smiled at me kindly and asked me to wait while his wife prepared the food.

I took a seat and enjoyed the wonderful smells coming from the kitchen. Before long the man called, "Your food's ready." He handed me a large plate containing not just my hamburger but also a pile of French fries and a big piece of fried chicken.

I was alarmed. "I didn't order all that," I said. "Just a hamburger."

He grinned. "It's on the house," he announced. I was flabbergasted, and I felt a little emotional. It was such an act of kindness out of the blue.

And that's how I met David and Mary Miller.

For some reason, David and Mary decided to take me under their wing, and, just like that, I went from not belonging to belonging. They treated me like a member of their family—as if I were one of their own children. I was made to feel like a big brother to their three younger kids.

Later, when I asked them what compelled them to befriend an immigrant, they assured me that they had no such plan in mind. They just liked me and enjoyed being around me. Mary teased me that she was impressed that I wiped off the table after I was done eating. "No American student does that!" she said.

I was left with the realization that if you're lucky, you form relationships that change your life. And I was very lucky because I wanted to immerse myself in my new country and learn everything I could and the Millers were happy to oblige. David made a point of teaching me about my new country and helping me navigate it. He wouldn't allow me to isolate myself. He'd show up at the library where I was studying and announce, "We're going out. Close your books." We'd get in his car, and we'd drive around, seeing the sights. On several occasions, he took me into Kansas City, and I marveled at the beautiful Spanish-style architecture and the lavish fountains. Once he drove me to a small town a couple hours away that had been devastated by a tornado. I had never seen that level of natural destruction before.

I was hungry for knowledge. I kept a little notebook with me and wrote down all the new words I learned.

Driving in the countryside one day, I said, "Wow, look at all these cows." David said, "Oh, no, Paul, we don't call them cows. We call them *Angus*." I dutifully wrote "Angus" in my little notebook.

David also helped me get established. I needed a car, but I didn't have any credit to get a loan. David knew how hard it was to get that first credit. He took me to see the local Chrysler dealer, and with David's assurances, he was happy to give me credit. That was an important milestone.

David was something of a jack-of-all-trades. In addition to the restaurant, he had a furniture store, and he also sold advertising for a radio station. One day he asked whether I'd like to go along on a business call to a car dealership where he was selling radio time. I appreciated David's taking me, and I realized it took some guts to introduce me to the good old boys in local business.

We walked into the dealer's office, and David told him I was a student. The dealer said hello and then didn't pay any further attention to me. I just watched David in action, thinking, this is how you do a sales call. David had told me before that he didn't know the guy. They were complete strangers, but David treated him like an old friend.

The first thing he did was launch into a discussion about how the fish weren't biting, and the guy was nodding his head and agreeing, and David told him about another lake where the fishing was better. Then David started asking him about his son's baseball team. They didn't get down to business until the end of the conversation, and very shortly after we walked out with the ad buy.

After we left, I asked David how he knew to talk to the guy about fishing and baseball. He laughed. "Easy. It's all about being observant. He's got a couple fish on the wall, a picture of his son in a baseball uniform."

David explained that doing business was all about relationships. "Just make sure people like you and make sure you're likable," he told me. He was the first person ever to give me that advice, and it proved to be the most important advice I ever received.

I skipped the first summer term in school and drove to San Francisco with four other guys. I shared a small apartment with eight people and got a job as a busboy at a restaurant on Fisherman's Wharf. I earned pretty good money with tips, but I had to take a tablecloth back to the apartment to use as a blanket. By the end of the summer, I'd made enough money to buy a very small diamond. I flew back to Taiwan, and Maggie and I got married. She returned with me to the United States. We were so excited to be together, to start a new life. It was a wonderful adventure for us. When you're young, you're not afraid.

We flew to San Francisco and then drove cross-country to Missouri. We saw the vastness of the landscape and enjoyed all the different kinds of food.

We spent a lot of time in gas stations and had at least two flat tires. People were very friendly. When we got close to Denver, I called David.

"Paul, we were starting to get worried!" he exclaimed. "Where are you?" I told him we'd decided to drive so I could show Maggie this great country. "We'll be arriving around midnight tomorrow," I said. "I wanted to ask you whether we could come there until we get our student housing settled."

"Of course," he said instantly. "We'll keep a light on."

We lived in David and Mary's basement for a few weeks and applied for married housing. Eventually, we were given a tiny trailer, no bigger than 12 by 40. As we were moving in, along came Mary with pots and pans and towels and blankets and other basic supplies. David and Mary gave Maggie a job in their restaurant, and she began to learn English.

We were often invited to join the Miller family for meals. Maggie was still learning about American cuisine, and she didn't really like it. Mary would tell her the same thing she told her children when they didn't want to try something new: "Just take three bites." So Maggie forced herself to do that.

One day when we were invited over to the Miller house, Maggie brought a plastic container. "What's that?" I asked. She gave me a mysterious smile. When we walked into the kitchen, Maggie opened the container. "It's pork belly," she told David and Mary. They recoiled, and Mary grinned. "Just three bites," she said. They had no choice. But I could tell they were choking it down. They didn't really like pork belly.

One evening, I was in the library studying and there was a big storm brewing. Someone mentioned the threat of a tornado, and I jumped up, alarmed. Maggie was alone in the trailer, and I knew that trailers were always the most vulnerable in a tornado. I ran for the door, and one of the guards stopped me. I said, "I need to go home." He tried to talk me out of leaving and said, "It's very dangerous out there." I said, "I have to get home because my wife is in the trailer."

I ran to my 1959 Chevrolet Impala and drove to our trailer. The sky was black, and the air was heavy with the approaching storm. When I arrived at the trailer, I found it empty. Maggie wasn't there. David had already picked her up and taken her to safety.

They took care of us. That's what family does, David said. That's how I realized that we were like family. We stayed close friends through all the coming decades. They were proud of my success, and we loved each other. After we moved to Florida, David and Mary would visit us sometimes, and we would visit them in Missouri. They would always be like family to us.

TODAY I LISTEN TO the immigration debate, and I realize that for many Americans who have just heard the rhetoric without having a personal experience, the concept of immigration is remote and negative. So I ask myself, What is *my* concept—how do I see it through the prism of my own experience, and how does that apply today?

To tell the truth, after 38 years here, I don't look at myself and think, "I am a Chinese American." I think, "I am an American." My children don't think of themselves as Chinese Americans. They are Americans. But there's more to it than that.

I've heard people voice the complaint about immigrants that they "stick to their own" and don't assimilate. That hasn't been my experience. Living in northwest Florida, we didn't know many Asians, and we wanted to become Americanized. But that doesn't mean we abandoned our Chinese roots. Maggie became the keeper of the culture. She made sure our children knew and appreciated their heritage. We realized that embracing our past did not take away from our Americanness.

One hundred years ago, the immigrants who came here wanted to be 100 percent assimilated. They knew they were here to stay. There was no chance of traveling back and forth. But I think today America is richer because of the cultural infusion.

Maggie and I own a co-op apartment in Flushing, a bustling neighborhood in Queens, New York, which is a virtual Chinatown. The streets are thronged with Chinese, and there are many restaurants serving authentic cuisine. I love to take my Western friends and colleagues for dinner at these restaurants, where they always fall in love with the food and the atmosphere.

If you visit our home, Maggie will cook a huge spread—fragrant bowls of steaming beef soup followed by heaping platters of crispy duck, stir-fried chicken and vegetables, steamed pork buns, bowls of rice. She inherited her cooking skills from her mother, Fu Pei Mei, who was a culinary celebrity in Taiwan for many years. Her television show, *Fu Pei Mei's Time*, was so popular that many people compared her to Julia Child. She was the author of more than 50 cookbooks, and Maggie spent much time in the kitchen with her mother. Those of us who have been lucky enough to dine at her table are grateful for that.

I believe that every immigrant who comes to America is proud of his or her heritage. I am well aware of the gift this country has given me and my family. But I have also given a gift in return. I care more about the United States than anywhere else. This is my home, and I've always done everything I could to make it better.

My Taiwanese culture places great emphasis on achievement over ethnicity, so embracing America was easy for me. I was drawn to the inge-nuity and dedication of the people I worked with. I treasured the warmth of relationships that was freely offered. It didn't take long for America to feel like home to me.

People often ask me what I think about the current immigration debate. Do I support comprehensive immigration reform? Am I in favor of the DREAM Act? What do I think about stronger border control? These are complicated issues. But my belief is that immigration is the cornerstone to American greatness. I share the view that Thomas Friedman expressed in an op-ed column titled "America's Real Dream Team." He wrote, "I am a pro-immigration fanatic. I think keeping a constant flow of legal immigrants in our country—whether they wear blue collars or lab coats—is the key to keeping us ahead. Because when you mix all of these energetic, high-aspiring people with a democratic system and free markets, magic happens. If we hope to keep that magic, we need immigration reform that guarantees that we will always attract and retain, in an orderly fashion, the world's first-round aspirational and intellectual draft choices."

We often talk about the concept of American exceptionalism, meaning that this country is fundamentally different from others—not just in our form of government but also in the character of the people.

So here is what I believe about the immigration debate:

- I believe that we should encourage the best and brightest from other countries to make a home here and contribute to the building of our prosperity and our character. As Friedman put it, these are the number one "draft choices."

- I believe that we should continue to make it easier for the family members of immigrants to come here, because family values and family stability are the foundation of a strong nation.

- I believe that the DREAM Act supports our basic American principles of fairness and opportunity. For all practical purposes, these kids are Americans, and this is their home.

- I believe it is important for us to have strong borders and to control the flow of people into the country, but, at the same time, we should make it possible for those who have aspirations and ambitions to be part of our great, diverse land.

In *That Used to Be Us: How America Fell Behind the World It Invented and How We Can Come Back*, Thomas Friedman and Michael Mandelbaum point out that American exceptionalism isn't an entitlement. It doesn't come automatically from doing nothing. We have to earn our exceptionalism with action. That means opening ourselves up to the vibrant and complicated new world we face. It means having an opportunity-based, not a fear-based, immigration policy. It means taking advantage of the talents of the world to make ourselves stronger and more competitive.

There are many politicians who view immigrants as "takers," not "makers." That hasn't been my experience. And many experts agree. Economists report that immigrants are a net positive for the economy. Research by UCLA Professor Raúl Hinojosa-Ojeda shows that legalizing our nation's undocumented immigrant population and reforming our legal immigration system would add a cumulative $1.5 trillion to the gross domestic product over a decade. Part of the benefit comes from the DREAM Act. Research by Notre Dame economists Juan Carlos Guzmán and Raúl Jara finds that the economic benefit of the DREAM Act could be as high as $329 billion by 2030. With legitimacy come better education and training and higher-paying jobs. It's a win-win for everyone.

Today, our colleges and universities are bursting with talented students from countries all over the world. They're taking advantage of our fine education system to advance their own dreams and prospects. What a shame if all that talent leaves America at the end of the school term. Instead, we should welcome them to stay here and build America.

three

CAN ANYONE STILL MAKE IT IN AMERICA?

When I was five years old, my mother asked me, "What do you want to be when you grow up?" I told her very seriously, "I want to be the head of a factory." She started laughing. She thought it was very cute, because I was such a small boy. But it meant something to me. In Chinese, the word for the manager of a plant is *chang zhang. Chang* means "factory," and *zhang* means "head." Some little boys want to be scientists, some engineers, some heads of state. For me, being a *chang jiang* was the perfect idea. I loved getting my hands dirty. I loved creating things—carving pieces of wood or cutting stone.

If I had stayed in Taiwan, perhaps I would have run a factory somewhere, but that was doubtful because our future was so constrained. You had to know someone to get a good job; you had to be connected in order to advance. It was not a meritocracy. No parent ever told a child, "You can be anything you want to be."

In the United States, I understood that my education meant something. So with my master's in industrial management and systems engineering, I soon had a big opportunity to consider—an offer from Harris Corporation in Florida, the third-largest defense contractor after Lockheed and Boeing.

At the time, I was working at Chesebrough-Ponds as an industrial engineer, handling work flow, cost control, and labor relations. For a young engineer, labor relations was like being thrown into the lion's den. I learned so much about dealing with people: how to listen, how to negotiate, how to handle conflicts. It would be invaluable experience. Maggie and I now had two small children, Jessica and John. (Our third child, Jennifer, wouldn't arrive for another couple years.) My mother, who was now a widow, was living with us and helping with the kids. Maggie and my mother were a very enthusiastic cheering section, so when I told them about the offer from Harris, they were excited. I think they would have been happy no matter what I decided to do, but none of us liked the cold Missouri winters, so a move to Florida was especially welcome. "We'll have oranges!" my mother cried happily. So off we went to the Sun Belt.

Harris was located in Fort Walton Beach, on North Florida's Gulf coast, surrounded by glittering emerald waters and miles of powdery white beaches. It was somewhat unknown to most people, who think of Florida as being Miami, West Palm Beach, or Orlando. But it was a sprawling and relatively prosperous place because it housed Eglin Air Force Base, one of the largest bases in the country, which spanned more than 700 square miles.

We were attracted by the beauty, the warm climate, and the cozy suburban neighborhoods, which seemed a perfect and safe place to raise a family. We found a modest home on a quiet, winding street, with the elementary school a short walk through a park behind our house. It seemed the ideal location to raise our children. I would start my first company in the garage of that house, and we would stay in that home until our first daughter left for college.

I was in charge of the production engineering at Harris. I was also in charge of the quality control for government support systems and weapons testing systems. The next few years were happy ones.

Then, in 1989, the Berlin Wall came down, ending the Cold War. Whenever there is a change in military priorities, it affects the support systems. Our boss, John Brinkley, came to us and said, "I have good news and bad news. The bad news is that Harris is going to close our division in Florida. The good news is that you'll all have a job in Syosset, New York."

I didn't really want to move. My family was happy in Florida. I thought long and hard. Could I build my own company from the tinkering I was doing in my garage? Maggie didn't hesitate. She encouraged me. She was completely unafraid of what the future would bring.

I went to John, and I told him, "Thank you for your offer of a job in New York, but I've decided to start my own company." He stared at me for a moment without expression, and then he turned around and walked out of the room.

I felt bad about his reaction. We'd always had a good relationship, and I hated that I'd let him down. But it didn't change my mind.

A day passed, and then on the second day, John walked into my office. He sat down and apologized for his reaction. "I'll miss you, Paul," he said, "but if this is what you want to do, you should do it." Then he told me the reason for his strong reaction. "Many years ago, some friends invited me to join them in a start-up, and I didn't do it. It was a company called Texas Instruments. I didn't take the opportunity. Go for it. And if you want to come back, all you have to do is give me a call."

I have to say that I started my company not because I had a dream but because I realized that if I worked for myself, I could never be laid off.

I knew I could always get a job, but I wanted to be independent—to grow based on my own merits and ingenuity.

Now I was on my own, and the first couple of years were very, very difficult. I was just trying to survive. I was trying to build my company around things I knew how to do. I used to joke to Maggie that if I'd known how to cook fried rice, I would have opened a Chinese restaurant. But what I knew how to do was electronics—in particular, mapping the life cycle of components and solving problems for large systems. Life cycle management is very important and very complex. It involves assuring the sustainability of a product from cradle to grave. The details can be mind-numbing. Consider that even the smallest component on an aircraft has 20 smaller components and you begin to see how extensive the plan has to be. It's like a family tree for a large family.

I was working night and day, but it would take three and a half years before I got anywhere. That was a low point of my life. We had very little savings, and we were struggling. During that time, Maggie got her job at Pizza Hut. There were so many times I said, "Oh, hell, I can't do this. I'm going to go get a real job." And the only voice that kept me going, the only support I had, was Maggie. She always gave me a boost of confidence at the critical moment when I needed it. She'd say, "Let's try it a little longer and see what happens." And I'd keep going.

One day, John Brinkley called me. He asked, "Paul, your wife works at Pizza Hut?" He sounded very concerned.

"Yeah," I admitted. I was embarrassed.

"Send her to me," he said. He wanted to give her a job.

Later, I found out what had happened. Stan Davis, a vice president at Harris and a great guy who had been something of a mentor to me, had burst into John's office, quite agitated. "I just had lunch at Pizza Hut, and Maggie Hsu was working there," he said. "You have to hire her. Those kids need to have health insurance."

So John went to my old colleague Keith Biggs and said, "Find Maggie a job. Make it happen." Keith was in the middle of downsizing, not adding employees. But he didn't hesitate. Maggie was hired on the spot.

I felt as if a hand had reached out and pulled us out of the water just as we were drowning. Maggie went to work for Harris on second shift, which started at 2:00 in the afternoon. She trained to solder on circuit boards. She was so good at it that I had her do some work for me.

Once again, I discovered the importance of relationships. Keith had become a close friend. He'd stayed on at Harris to help with the drawdown, and he was interested in what I was doing in my little garage. One day, he called me. "Paul," he said, "we have all this equipment in storage. I thought you might be able to use some of it."

"I have no money," I protested.

He shrugged it off. "Use what you need," he offered.

In important ways, my friends and colleagues rescued me when I needed rescuing. My confidence was building. I was beginning to see a pathway to succeed. I figured I could build things cheaper and faster than a company such as Boeing could build them in their facility just because I was small. I could move faster. I was a small boat compared to the *Titanic*. That was my advantage. I could maneuver in times of crisis.

I knew it would take a few years of struggle, but I believed I could do it. It was all about working harder and being able to recognize opportunities. I had no idea of the real challenges I would face. Sometimes ignorance is a blessing, because you're not crippled by fear.

AS I WAS STRUGGLING to get my company off the ground, someone suggested I attend a vendor's conference. I paid $200 to get a little booth, and Maggie and I manned it. While we were there, I accidentally over-heard a conversation between two McDonnell Douglas engineers. They were discussing a big problem with the relay module for the A-12, which was a new navy fighter jet. In the design, they had put all the relays in one small panel, and that was not feasible because if a single bullet hit that panel, the whole plane was gone. They were quite worried about the flaw.

I got up my nerve and walked over and introduced myself to the head engineer. I shook his hand and gave him my card and told him a little about my business. I didn't say I'd overheard them discussing the relay panel. But when I got home, I wrote him a letter saying I had a solution.

It was quite simple, actually. Instead of putting all the relays in one panel, I suggested making 25 relay module assemblies and spreading them out. That way, if one panel were hit, it wouldn't bring down the plane.

He wrote back and said he liked my idea. Could I build a prototype? Of course!

We got on the phone and started discussing the details. He asked, "How much will it cost for you to build me five different sets?"

I did a quick calculation. "Probably about $2,000 each, so $10,000."

He started laughing. "You don't understand," he said. "We are McDonnell Douglas. We can't do contracts for anything less than $50,000."

I didn't know. I had no idea how to negotiate as a small business with such a big contractor. So I said, "OK, I'll build you more of them." That's how I got started with McDonnell Douglas.

We worked on the program for about a year, and one day I got a call from the project manager. It was a difficult time for McDonnell Douglas, and he told me they were discontinuing the A-12. "When can you shut down production?" he asked.

I didn't let him hear the worry in my voice. I told him we could shut down by the end of the week, and we wouldn't charge them after that. I could have delayed the shutdown longer and tried to extract more money. But I had taught myself to always take the long view. I sensed how urgent this was for him, and I wanted to be his ally, not a difficult subcontractor. He was immensely relieved that I could shut down so quickly.

But my mind was working on how to rescue the business. McDonnell Douglas was a big company with many other jets besides the A-12. I began to talk about how we might use the relay assembly on other equipment. He hadn't thought about that, but he was immediately interested. Five years later, our relay model assembly was on every McDonnell Douglas fighter jet. So I lost one piece of business but gained so much more.

I WAS ESTABLISHING A FOOTHOLD, but I still didn't have the wherewithal to build my company. I religiously studied the Department of Defense requirements. Absolute transparency was necessary if you were to buy an airplane or a ship or do maintenance on the airplane or ship, because it was taxpayers who were footing the bill. Of course, I was too small to build an airplane or a ship. But I was big enough to build a cable or a support system. By now, I was concerned with more than survival; I wanted to grow my company—to make a difference. I saw that the DOD wanted someone to design and build an underwater sonar detector. I requested the requirements from the Naval Coastal System Center in Panama City, Florida.

I needed a team, but I didn't have the money to pay salaries for the high-level designers I needed. So, once again, I turned to my relationships. I called Keith and several others who were still working at Harris, and I asked them whether they'd like to come over to my house a couple nights a week and sit around the kitchen table and talk about a project I wanted to do. I promised to feed them Maggie's legendary Chinese meals.

I got an enthusiastic response. I told them I couldn't pay them, but they wanted to do it. I think there were two reasons for this: One, they liked me. I was blessed with a likability that has served me well all my life. I care about people. I'm a relationship builder. Two, they were engineers. Solving problems and inventing designs was what they loved to do. So my deal was that they would help me, and if I got the contract, I'd pay them. Meanwhile, they'd eat some fine meals.

So they came—and word got out, and others wanted to come. Twice a week, I had at least three or four top-notch engineers in my dining room working on drawings. It was fun for them. By the time we were done, I had a plan that was as sophisticated as any you'd ever seen.

The navy had scheduled a dealer's conference, where companies that wanted to build the underwater sonar detector would show their stuff.

When it was my turn, I asked for an easel. They were surprised. "Why do you want an easel?" they asked. I said, "Because I've got something to show you guys."

I put up the drawings. "If I get the contract, this is the way I'm going to build it," I said. As I outlined my plan, I could see they were leaning forward, very interested. My team and I had thought of everything.

When I'd finished, the head guy cleared his throat. "So, what company did you say you were with?" he asked. They'd never heard of me before.

"I'm with Manufacturing Technology," I said. "We're located in Fort Walton Beach."

"How many people do you have?"

"We have a few good engineers," I said evasively. I shaded the truth just a little. After all, how could we have designed such a great plan if we didn't have good engineers?

I could see that they were very interested. They asked whether I could leave the plans with them. I agreed but asked them to sign a nondisclosure clause, which took some nerve, but I didn't want anyone else using my designs or doing something similar but cheaper. They signed the nondisclosure agreement, and I left feeling the meeting had gone well.

About a week and a half later, I got a call from the project manager. "We liked your design," he said. "And your cost is in the ballpark. I just want to make sure that you agree to build this thing for $280,000."

I told him I could. "So, am I selected?" I asked.

He said they'd looked at a couple of other firms but had chosen me. I was so proud and happy, but there was no time for celebration. The contract was a victory, but that's when my troubles really started.

I needed capital to fulfill the contract. They weren't giving me money up front. I assumed that having the contract would be sufficient to get a loan. I was wrong. "You can't use the contract as collateral," my banker told me. "It's just a piece of paper. There's no guarantee that you're going to deliver."

I started pounding the pavement. I visited every bank from Fort Walton Beach to Pensacola, trying to get a loan. And every bank had the same response—no. The reality was beginning to hit me. I had a life-changing contract with the government, but I didn't have the resources to fulfill it.

One morning, after yet another rejection, I was sitting in a coffee shop and feeling completely discouraged. I was at the end of the line. By nature, I'm an optimistic guy, but I couldn't see any hope. I had run out of options.

While I was sitting there, a local banker named Skip Reinert walked in and saw me. I knew Skip, and we were somewhat friendly. He took one look at my slumped shoulders and asked, "Who died?"

I spilled out my story, but instead of commiserating, he shook his head in amazement. "Hasn't anyone told you about the government small business loan program?" he asked. No one had.

Skip went to work putting me in touch with the right people, and I learned about the SBA guaranty loan. The government and the Small Business Administration guarantee 85 percent of a bank's loan, lowering the risk from 100 percent to 15 percent. Now Skip's bank, First National Bank, was willing to give me the loan.

Through the SBA guaranty loan program, I learned about another government program called the 8(a) Business Development Program. It is an essential instrument for helping socially and economically disadvantaged entrepreneurs gain access to the economic mainstream of American society. This program helped me tremendously. I'll talk more about that later.

At the time of my first big contract, I didn't exactly have a facility for such an ambitious project. I had a small office in Valparaiso in a run-down shopping center next to a Chinese restaurant. But I knew people. When I'd worked at Harris, I had given contracts to many local companies, and the relationships I'd built were golden. I started making calls. I called different companies, different people, using their backyards, using their equipment and forklifts. I borrowed someone's big yard to build the thing. We succeeded. That project really launched my business. Now I was an official government contractor, and the sky was the limit.

I WAS LUCKY. But when people ask, "Can anyone make it in America?" I realize that success is much more than luck. It's also more than just hard work. You have to be smart. As my father always admonished me as a child, "Don't eat something that doesn't smell good."

I also believe that one of the keys to my success is imagination. I can sense the opportunities. I see possibilities that others may not see. I always had a strong drive, and I poured my heart and soul into building my business. However, it wasn't a magical process.

You have to start with core principles, which become the building blocks of everything you do. My four core principles are integrity, customer orientation, innovation, and commitment. Integrity—that is, doing the right thing—is number one. That's how you ensure longevity in a business. Second, focusing on the customers ensures that you're always thinking ahead, identifying their needs and changing as they change. I wasn't interested in creating business plans that would be obsolete almost as soon as they were written. Innovation was a constant. Commitment extended not only to working hard but also to really caring. I believed that a good manager had to have a big heart—big enough to recognize that the people who share the pain are entitled to share the gain.

When you start your own business, it's no longer an eight-hour job. It's 24 hours a day, seven days a week. You think about your business all the time, even in your sleep.

My business was growing. I now had 50 people working for me. That meant payroll every two weeks. Payroll is everything. I remember Mitt Romney, in the 2012 presidential campaign, talking about how he understood how to build the economy because he'd met payroll. Every business owner knew what he was talking about. Meeting payroll is the crucible. It makes you strong, and you have to have a solid relationship with your bank.

I'll never forget one experience that really had me sweating. It was Thursday. Payroll was Friday. And I was short. I had a line of credit, so I called my banker and asked whether I could get money transferred into my account for Friday's payroll. He said he'd check and get back to me.

I waited all afternoon. No call. I called him again. He wasn't there. Dinnertime came, and we were supposed to go out. I couldn't tear myself away from the phone. I waited and waited and sweated and sweated. That evening, I called the banker at home. He wasn't home.

I lay in bed awake all night long. It drove Maggie crazy. "Go to sleep," she urged. But I couldn't sleep. What would I tell my employees when they didn't get their checks? It was unthinkable.

I got up early, and at 6:30 a.m., I called the banker at home. As I was stumbling through my apologies for calling him so early, he laughed. "Oh, Paul, I'm sorry. I forgot to call you back. The money was transferred yesterday."

FINALLY, I REALIZED MY childhood dream. I ran a factory. I was *chang jiang*. Actually, it was more than a factory. MTI became a thriving business, and I was able to buy property and expand rapidly. I invited David and Mary to come to Florida and be there the day I broke ground on my factory. They had tears in their eyes. We all did.

Once the factory was up and running, every time I walked in the door, I felt my blood pressure rising—in a good way. I'd look around and I'd see people moving and machines operating, and it made me so proud. My feelings went beyond accomplishment. It was an organic thing. This place was part of me.

I owe much of my success to the fact that so many people really wanted to see me make it. I had a solid cheering section, and I always emphasized that the strength of my company was its people. You can always buy or rent facilities and equipment, but it takes time and effort to acquire and develop good people. I wanted every customer who had a contact with our company to come away feeling happy and in good hands.

Relationships, as I've said, are the most important thing in the world. I never forgot that day long ago when David took me along on a client call. I noticed his demeanor, his ability to relate to the customer as an individual—to show respect. In business, I always made sure to visit the different military bases at least once or twice a year. I'd tell them that these were just routine visits, to make sure that we were serving them well. They liked it, because these were the people doing the work. I didn't visit the two-star generals or the base commanders; I visited the section chiefs who were like midlevel managers. I realized that they had a lot of power because they chose the contractors. Instead of hobnobbing with the hierarchy, I went to the people who were in the trenches of the business.

One of these was Keith, my old colleague and friend from Harris. Keith finally finished downsizing the department, and he went to work as a consultant. I knew what a talented guy he was, and our philosophies were in sync. One day I ran into him on a plane from Boston, and I was so happy to see him. He was delighted to hear that my business was doing so well.

"Come to work for me," I said. I meant it. I'd be lucky to have a guy like Keith. He laughed. "You can't afford me," he said, and he was right. But happiness is about more than making money, and although Keith was well paid, he traveled so much that he didn't have time for his family. His wife wanted him to get a job locally. So, to my surprise and gratitude, he soon accepted my offer.

Keith is a big, good-natured Southern guy with great warmth and a sense of humor. He also has a brilliant mind. He helped me take my company to the next level, including starting a second company, Total Parts Plus, which we opened when we received a government contract to do component life cycle planning for the F-15 aircraft. It was a big risk to take on that project and start another company. Keith recognized the opportunity before anyone else.

Recognizing opportunities is a key to success—and that's why I am convinced that our country, in spite of the recent recession, is still a nation of great promise. I want young people to know that.

On May 7, 1991, I stood beside President George H. W. Bush, along with four other small business owners, in the Rose Garden. "Welcome to the White House, America's ultimate mom-and-pop operation," the president said in greeting us. It was Small Business Week, and the president had singled us out for special merit to receive the Small Business Person of the Year Award.

"There's an extraordinary force at work inside America," he said, "a force that does the good work of this country, a force that embodies America's can-do spirit. And that force, as we all know here today, is small business, made up of over 20 million men and women across the land who have taken control of their own lives, made their own choices and decisions; 20 million who stake out their goals and pursue them with determination and grit and vision; 20 million who believe in themselves, their neighbors, their country. And we're here today to celebrate these 20 million pieces of the American Dream."

I smiled at my wife and mother, who were there to cheer me on, and stepped forward to receive my award as the Small Business Prime Contractor of the Year. The president told those gathered that I embodied "courage . . . as an immigrant who left Taiwan in search of freedom and opportunity."

I cherished that award, and I appreciated the acknowledgment from the highest office in the land. I've always believed—and I've been lucky enough to prove it in my own life—that a big advantage in America is the chance to create a business from scratch. But when I received that award, I was just at the beginning of making my company happen.

Thomas Edison once said, "I never perfected an invention that I did not think about in terms of the service it might give others . . . I find out what the world needs, then I proceed to invent it." That's a philosophy I took to heart. I believe that America is an opportunity culture and there are always new businesses waiting to be created.

The point is that when you ask, "Can anyone make it in America?" the answer is yes. As long as there are needs to be met, there will be opportunities.

four

INDIVIDUALS IN SMALL BUSINESS: AMERICA'S BACKBONE AND HOPE

It's an enduring principle that small businesses are the backbone of the American economy. They are an expression of a core American ideal of independence and ingenuity, growing out of the pioneer spirit that built the nation.

Let's take a closer look at the characteristics of small businesses that make them the engine of our economy:

Small businesses are nimble. They can respond quickly to upturns and downturns in the economy. Business owners can make decisions and begin to implement plans very rapidly.

Small businesses are resilient. They tend to be need based. They can thrive even in hard times by focusing on needs in their areas.

Small businesses are community minded. They prosper in collaboration with local stakeholders and understand that this collaboration is the rising tide that helps lift all boats.

Every year the Small Business Administration hosts a competition for the Small Business Owner of the Year, and each state picks its own winner. These are not big stars whose names are on the lips of every American. They're ordinary people who do extraordinary things in their communities, and they possess great wisdom that stands the test of time and is as relevant today as it ever was. Here is some advice from recent winners:

- Don't be afraid.

- Take the high road.

- Surround yourself with great people.

- Find a mentor.

- Do what you say you're going to do.

- Be a good role model in your community.

- Prepare yourself mentally, physically, and spiritually.

- Be collaborative.

- Dream big and believe in yourself.

- Find ways to give back.

Even in the face of great challenges, small businesses remain optimistic. In February 2013, JPMorgan Chase surveyed more than 2,600 owners and leaders of businesses with annual revenue between $100,000 and $20 million to assess current business challenges, future expectations, and issues impacting their strategic decision making. Those who responded were mostly positive regarding their growth opportunities, with more than half reporting that they expect at least moderate growth in revenues in the coming year. How they make that happen is the main story of our times.

Being a small business owner requires leadership. The buck stops with you. But it also requires collaboration. There are helping hands reaching out to help. You just need to know where to look for them.

IN MY BUSINESS, A BREAKTHROUGH came when I was selected by Boeing (formerly McDonnell Douglas) along with two other small companies for mentor assistance under the Department of Defense's Mentor-Protégé Program. This program was launched in 1991 to support economically and socially disadvantaged small businesses. I was an immigrant, and I didn't have a lot of money in the bank, so I qualified. Boeing took me in, guided me, and educated me on the complicated world of military contracting. I was proud of this association, buoyed by the idea that they thought I was worth the effort.

That relationship greatly enhanced MTI's ability to design, fabricate, and test airborne avionics hardware. By sharing their expertise with us, Boeing helped us be better partners in their business. We had that rare and valuable business chemistry that makes relationships work to everyone's advantage.

The relationship with Boeing really flourished. In 2001, MTI became one of the 12 gold-level suppliers in the world for Boeing, which is the highest level you can achieve.

At that time, Boeing had 28,000 suppliers worldwide, but only 12 were selected as gold suppliers (the others being bronze and silver). There's a tremendous amount of responsibility that comes with that status. You have to maintain a 100 percent delivery schedule and achieve 100 percent quality goals. That means you have to be *perfect*. When you consider that MTI was delivering more than 2,500 pieces of critical fly hardware to Boeing every year, it was a real challenge to agree to perfection. But we did it. Boeing reached out, and just like other times in my career, it was a generous helping hand that made a big difference for me. In my gratitude to the

DOD and Boeing, I knew what I had to do. In 2002, I decided to "pay it forward"—to become a mentor company to other small businesses. I started my own mentor-protégé program.

I set up an exploratory committee and sent the word out. I was looking for very small companies in arenas that fit with our expertise. I wasn't pretending to be Boeing! But I knew I could help others take advantage of contract opportunities and train them just as I had been trained. I ended up selecting three diverse companies: one was General Precision Manufacturing, an African American–owned metal fabrication and services company; one was Epoch Software, an Asian American woman–owned software development company; and one was Muskogee Metalworks, a Native American metalworks company.

Working with Muskogee Metalworks was an amazing experience. I had wanted a Native American protégé, and the Muscogee Poarch Creek tribe was in nearby Alabama. I loved the idea of the tribe's rich history. You might say that the Native Americans are the only people in the country who *aren't* immigrants. The tribe can trace its origins in the southeastern United States as far back as 1500. They had a rich culture and built beautiful ceremonial complexes and pyramids along the rivers of the region.

Like many Native American communities, the Poarch Creek tribe struggled for stability and faced daunting socioeconomic barriers. Poverty is a continuing crisis on many Native American reservations. But I thought the Poarch Creek reservation was very well run—very committed to business success. The tribe was well organized and motivated to improve the conditions of its people. I thought they would make a very good mentor-protégé partner.

I went to the reservation and smoked a peace pipe with the chief. Then I took on their five-man metalworks shop as a protégé. I was dedicated to the idea of making the reservation a place of opportunity for the tribal youth. At the signing ceremony, the general manager, Mal McGhee, put it this way: "We want to be a leader for other tribes. We want this to be a success story—for everyone to look back and say this is the model. We hope to be able to tell our tribal youth that if they want to be engineers, they don't have to leave the reservation to find work."

MTI lent them our expertise in manufacturing technology and helped them secure a $47-million contract from the Army Simulation and Training Command to build and repair army tank simulators. By the end of the first year, they had expanded so much that they purchased a larger facility, an 88,000-square-foot shuttered plant in Atmore, Alabama. Muskogee Metalworks became one of the biggest economic boosts the tribe had seen in generations. It was a very satisfying task.

I learned a lot about the commitment involved in being a mentor. I developed great admiration for Robert Williams, the African American owner of General Precision Manufacturing, who was one of my first protégés. Robert had started his company in 1995 and ran it for several years as a one-man show before adding a handful of employees. Robert had struggled through some hard times. Within the first year of being a protégé, buoyed by training and a strategic plan, Robert secured quality assurance qualifications from the Department of Defense, which led to a contract. By the end of 2002, he was adding more employees and expecting to earn gross revenues of nearly $2 million. The icing on the cake was the announcement that the DOD had selected General Precision Manufacturing to receive its prestigious Nunn-Perry Award for outstanding performance as a protégé.

Then Robert died suddenly, shattering his family and putting his dream in jeopardy. We were all crushed by Robert's death. He had a lot of friends and supporters in our community.

I went to see Robert's wife, Myra. She was heartbroken but full of dignity. "Robert had a vision to provide jobs for people in the community and to leave his children a family business," she told me. "I wish there were a way to rescue his vision."

"The company doesn't have to close," I told her. "You are the owner. It's up to you to decide what you're going to do, but if you want to keep it going, I'll help you."

"Me?" It never occurred to her that she could take over her husband's company. I knew she was a very capable lady, and I thought she could do it. "I can't make your decision for you," I said, "but promise me you'll think about it."

Myra did think about it. She wasn't without skills. She was currently employed in a navy civil service job, and she knew something about military contracts. In her career, she'd been a supervisor and a manager, but it was highly unusual for a woman to be at the helm of a manufacturing company. Finally, she called me. "I'm going to do it," she said. "I'm going to step out on the brink. I have faith." I was thrilled, and I promised again that I would help her.

Four months later, Myra stood on a stage in Washington and accepted the Nunn-Perry Award on behalf of her husband and her company. "I didn't expect to be up here today," she said with emotion. "I thought I'd be in the audience watching my husband, Robert. I know he's watching, and I feel in my heart that he's proud of me."

My third protégé, Epoch Software Systems, an Asian American woman–owned company in Gulf Breeze, Florida, offered high-level expertise in solving software systems and logistics engineering problems. I worked with the owner, Renee de la Cruz, to initiate her into the military contract environment. Today, Epoch is a prime contractor with the U.S. military and is a thriving company.

The mentor-protégé program was very successful. It really made me proud. In 2004, we won the Department of Defense Outstanding Mentor-Protégé Award. We won not only as a protégé to Boeing but also as a mentor. That was one of the highlights of my life.

BY 2005, MTI HAD grown into a major company, worth more than $60 million—and that didn't even count Total Parts Plus, which we'd started in 2000 as a separate enterprise that allowed clients to track the shelf life of their parts and stock as needed. But we were seeing a change in the way contracts were being awarded. After the terrorist attack on September 11, there was money pouring into the defense industry, but the agencies pulling the strings were giving most of the business to the large contractors, believing them to be more cost-effective. Not as many contracts were flowing down to the smaller companies. I could also see that aerospace was going into the cycle. What I mean by that is the way, every 20 years or so, the pendulum swings and the belts tighten. It's just a fact. The handwriting was on the wall. I realized that I had to either join someone to become a bigger company or start acquiring other companies. At that point, I had 450 employees, but it wasn't big enough. I had to double my size in order to stay competitive.

Keith encouraged me to consider selling the company. "Now is the time," he said. I knew he was right. It was a wrenching decision. When you're a business owner who started in your garage and went through all the hardships I'd been through, it's almost like giving up one of your children. But I agreed. When MTC Technologies made an offer of $75 million, I decided to accept it. However, I had two conditions. The first was that they had to hire all of my people. I refused to walk away from them and leave them to fend for themselves. It was very important to me that they be secure. The second condition was that the company had to stay local. My business had become important to the local economy, and I didn't want to disrupt that. They agreed to both conditions.

Deciding to sell MTI was a bittersweet experience. I had always run my business like a family. I knew every one of my 450 employees by name, and I felt responsible for their well-being. Many of them had taken a chance on me when I was just starting out, and that meant everything to me. I was heartened that my employees would be taken care of—they'd even get to keep their seniority. In addition, maybe with a bigger footprint they'd have a greater chance of prospering. The day of the handover was very emotional. I teared up as I remembered those long years of struggle, the endless hours toiling away in my garage. I felt the way a parent feels when a beloved child leaves the nest—proud and hopeful but with a little hole in my heart.

Total Parts Plus wasn't part of the deal; it was a separate entity. So I still had a business to grow and many more opportunities to uncover. First, I was called upon to give back to the country that had given me so much.

IN 2007, SHORTLY AFTER I sold MTI, I received a call from Washington, D.C. President George W. Bush wanted to appoint me to the Small Business Administration as the associate administrator of the SBA's Office of Government Contracting and Business Development. As an immigrant who had benefitted so much from American opportunity, I felt honored to have the chance to make a larger contribution, and it was an area that meant so much to me—helping small businesses get their share of government contracts. I felt primed for the role because of how intimately I knew the SBA programs. The 8(a) and guaranty loan programs played an integral role in my business opportunity, and I knew how effective they were in helping entrepreneurs.

I decided to accept the job for a year and put Keith in charge of the company in my absence. This wasn't so hard for me. I completely trusted him. We were as close as brothers and had the same business values. I knew I could always count on Keith to run the company as if it were his own.

I wasn't at all worried about my business. My family was another matter. I knew I couldn't pressure Maggie to come with me. For one thing, it was going to be a short-term appointment, and I'd be working so hard I wouldn't have much spare time. Maggie had a full life in Fort Walton Beach.

We decided I would go alone and she would visit me regularly. I rented a small one-bedroom apartment and moved in.

I was naive. I didn't realize how much I depended on Maggie, both emotionally and in my day-to-day life. Maggie was my balance, and Washington, D.C., was completely devoid of balance. When people weren't physically working, they were talking about work or checking their BlackBerrys. It was obsessive and unhealthy. Looking back, I think if I were to do it again, I would try to create more normalcy in my life—maybe get a larger condo and bring Maggie with me.

Going from running a business to the massive Washington bureaucracy was no easy transition. I know that many people are cynical about Washington, but maybe they'd feel differently if they saw how hard everyone works—how committed people are to doing the job of the nation. We were all completely committed to making life better for the working citizens.

I think we need to give a little more credit to government officials, especially presidential appointees. Presidential appointees are not there for the money. They're there to make the country better. In particular, I was charged with increasing the percentage of government contracts for small businesses. When I arrived, the picture was not good. More than half of all agencies were failing to meet the small business contracting goal of 23 percent to small businesses. It just wasn't being taken seriously. I was determined to change the trend.

My schedule was crazy. There were meetings piled on meetings. I'd go from one meeting to the next all day long and into the evening. Everyone wanted me to hear what he or she had to say, and I wanted to hear it, but after many hours of meetings, I'd feel as if my head was going to explode.

Often, I'd be in my office late into the night. I could see the Capitol dome out my window, and as the hours passed and it got darker, I'd look out on the lighted dome and think, "I'm doing the work of the people. What I do matters." And I'd work even harder.

However, I have to say that going from the independence of running my own company to the huge bureaucracy of Washington, D.C., was no easy task. In my company, the buck stopped with me. If I made a decision, we could act on it that day. At the SBA, it was the opposite, and I didn't always understand why things needed to be so unwieldy. For example, I had four secretaries, and they all sat outside my office. Don't ask me why I needed four secretaries. I have no idea. It seemed to me that they didn't have anything to do half the time. One day as I was rushing to be on time for a meeting, I handed a report to one of them. "Can you make me 10 copies quickly? I'm running late," I told her. She looked at her watch. "I can do it in two minutes because I'm on a break," she said. So I took my paper to the Xerox machine and made my own copies. It really annoyed me. Mind you, it wasn't that she didn't want to help me—but the rules were the rules.

Although there are many dedicated people working in Washington, the problem is that those without a can-do attitude just languish there. You can't get rid of them. The only thing you can do if someone is really bad is promote him or her and move him or her out of your section. Then you've made a worse problem for somebody else.

My time at the SBA was challenging—especially when I had to testify before Congress. I testified twice in the House and once in the Senate. I remember well the first time I testified in the U.S. Senate before the Committee on Small Business and Entrepreneurship. The hearing room was crowded, and the senators sat arrayed at an imposing bench at the front. I had seen hearings on television, and there I was, Paul Hsu, speaking to senators that were well known to most Americans—John Kerry (the chairman of the committee), Tom Harkin, Carl Levin, Olympia Snowe, and others. I wanted them to hear me from the standpoint of my immigrant roots and also from the standpoint of my experience as a small businessman. This is what I told them:

> As a first-generation immigrant myself, in 1984, I started my first high-tech company. After my company won the first contract, we needed working capital, money to buy parts, and material. Fortunately, I was able to find the finance I needed with the help of an SBA loan guarantee, and this was how I first came to know the agency. Later, my company was certified to participate in SBA's 8(a) program. My company is an example of the power of this program to give businesses opportunity to grow.
>
> SBA helped me to develop a successful business. It provided me with the access to capital, training, the development experience, and solid competitive opportunities. Simply put, without the agency, I could not have come this far. So it is absolutely an honor and privilege, Mr. Chairman, for me to join an agency that I truly, truly believe in.

I went on to describe the initiatives I believed would help us succeed at our mission. The senators asked many questions. They held my feet to the fire about what we were going to do to increase government contracts to our stated goal of 23 percent and what we were going to do to make sure that women had more opportunities. It was a grueling day, but I felt energized. I had real answers, and, for once, the bureaucratic impossibilities seemed to recede in that hearing room.

I did butt heads with Congress a bit over the issue of women. Absolutely on board with helping women-owned businesses, I agreed that there was a glass ceiling. But, if you put women in the same category as socially and economically disadvantaged people, it dilutes the impact, because women own about 60 percent of small businesses. They're not a minority per se. Plus, the figures involving women-owned business were somewhat contradictory. Although women-owned businesses were underrepresented in more than half of the industry categories, when the dollar value of the federal contracts was used as the measurement standard, they found little evidence that women-owned small businesses were underrepresented. However, I strongly voiced our commitment to make sure women got a fair shot at contracts—and we did create the Women-Owned Small Business Federal Contract Assistance Program, which would award women-owned businesses at least 5 percent of prime contracts while subcontracting dollars for each industry category, such as manufacturing, construction, education services, and health care.

I had so much to do at the SBA—so many reports, so many studies, so much paper—it was sometimes difficult to see where I was helping. One thing I did do, which I'm proud of to this day, was create the Scorecard Program to monitor all of the bureaucracies. This annual assessment tool helped to corral the bureaucracy. Scorecard measured how well federal agencies reached their small business and socioeconomic prime contracting and subcontracting goals. It included goals for small businesses, small businesses owned by women, small disadvantaged businesses, service-disabled veteran-owned small businesses, and small businesses located in historically underutilized business zones (HUBZones).

Not everyone liked the Scorecard system, because it was a pretty strict form of accountability. But I honestly believed it was the only way to hold them accountable and get those contracts increased. I'm proud to say that the Scorecard is still being used today.

Overall, my experience in Washington was worth it. I'm a big supporter of the idea that we should bring more businesspeople into government. We can provide a reality check in the nation's capital. Speaking for myself, it was an honor and a duty to serve in the government for a year. I hope my being there made a difference.

ONE LESSON I LEARNED in Washington was that in spite of how much politicians talk about the importance of developing small businesses, there is a big gap between rhetoric and reality. Small businesses (defined as businesses with fewer than 500 employees) were hurt more than anyone else by the financial crisis of 2008. They are always more vulnerable to acts of God such as hurricanes and tornados. They are subject to local economies that are beyond their control. When banks stop lending, small businesses are hurt more than anyone else.

The Center for Excellence in Service, which produces annual reports on the status of small businesses, reports that the competitive health of small businesses is the lowest it has been since the survey began. Nevertheless, it reports that the future is promising if only we embrace the challenge as a nation. That begins with appreciating the vital role of small businesses in our economy.

There are almost 28 million small businesses in the United States, and more than 22 million people are self-employed with no additional payroll or employees. In fact, 120 million people—more than 50 percent of the population—work in small businesses. These companies have been responsible for virtually all the growth in the past 20 years. While big business eliminated four million jobs, small businesses added eight million new jobs.

It may surprise you to know that creating a small business isn't solely a young person's game. In 2013, AARP reported that one in four people between ages 47 and 70 intend to start a business within the next five to 10 years, with 100,000 so-called encore entrepreneurs entering the small business environment in the next year. These older, more experienced workers bring a depth of knowledge of both business and the world that can make the small business climate only richer.

Once again, immigrants are front and center in this picture of prosperity. That translates into more than one in six small business owners in the United States being immigrants, according to the latest information gathered by the study—even as they make up just 13 percent of the overall population.

With immigrant business ownership come jobs and income. An estimated 4.7 million U.S. workers are employed by immigrant-owned firms gathering some $776 billion in revenues.

According to the Fiscal Policy Institute, the specific types of businesses most owned by immigrants are restaurants, real estate firms, grocery stores, and physician's offices. The top countries of birth for immigrant business owners include Mexico first, followed by India, South Korea, Cuba, China, Vietnam, Canada, and Iran.

An interesting note: the gender gap is slightly better among immigrants, with 29 percent of immigrant businesses owned by women compared to the average of 28 percent among U.S.-born females.

I often look at my sister Angela as a model of individual tenacity and ingenuity. Angela came to the United States before I did. She became an American citizen and had two children, and she and her husband lived a nice life. Then they got divorced, and Angela had to find a way to fend for herself.

She decided to pursue a career in real estate, and while she studied for the broker's exam, she took on small jobs to keep going—such as hosing down ice cream trucks at the end of the day. She was paid $10 per truck.

When I first arrived in the United States, I went to visit Angela, and she had just passed the broker's exam. She showed me the book, and I looked inside. Above every line of text, Angela had translated it into Chinese in her neat handwriting. She told me it was the only way she could understand every word. She was trying to impress upon me that it wasn't easy, but she made it because she worked hard.

Angela did well as a real estate broker, and in the 1980s during the real estate boom, she became a developer. She'd buy a piece of property, subdivide it, and hire all the contractors to build beautiful units. She did very well, but, in many respects, Angela's is a typical immigrant story. She would tell you that she succeeded because she had no choice. There was no fallback option. Angela *had* to be successful—and she *was* successful.

If I were to pinpoint the three most important factors that lead to success for small businesses, they would be:

1. Small businesses need a fair shot at government contracts.

According to a project cosponsored by the Brookings Institution and the Small Business Administration, if the federal government increased its percentage of spending with American small businesses from 23 percent to 30 percent, the result would be an additional $100-billion investment into the American economy annually.

The SBA offers a full range of services, including an excellent online Government Contracting Classroom, designed to help small businesses understand how the government buys goods and services. The course describes prime and subcontracting assistance programs; SBA certification programs; and special programs for women, veterans, and underserviced groups, including immigrants.

There is also information about the SBA's Mentor-Protégé Program where businesses can seek the following benefits: technical and management assistance, prime contracting opportunities, and financial assistance in the form of equity or loans. This is a case where the government is there to help businesses.

2. Small businesses need access to capital.

I spoke earlier about the SBA 8(a) Business Development Program that gave me a leg up when I needed it. I suspect that many eligible small businesses don't know about this program. The 8(a) program offers many kinds of assistance to companies that are owned by socially and economically disadvantaged individuals. It enables struggling upstarts to enter the mainstream of the American economy. For example, in 2012, nearly 5,000 small businesses received more than $1.8 billion in federal government grants and contracts to help them carry out the R&D necessary to develop and bring high-tech products to market.

Recalling my own start in business, I scrambled for every dollar. One avenue that wasn't available then but is proliferating now is microfinancing. The idea of microfinancing actually had its origin in aid to underdeveloped countries when it was found that tiny loans of as little as $25 could help impoverished people start businesses such as creating a fish stand, selling handmade jewelry, or opening a small convenience store. Today, microlenders are springing up all over the United States to provide small loans for very small businesses that are not eligible for conventional business loans. These loans can be as little as $10,000. Many of these microlenders are small banks that serve immigrant communities almost exclusively. For example, Noah Bank in New York City caters to the Korean American community. Cameo, a microlending support company, has arranged loans for more than 21,000 businesses in California—such as organic farm stands, childcare centers, and food trucks.

3. Small businesses need ongoing training and support.

The SBA has a number of programs that help train small business owners for success. Many of these training sessions can be conducted online through the Small Business Learning Center. Examples of classrooms include how to start a franchising business, how to write a business plan, how to create an accounting system, how to market your business, and more. One program that is very promising is the SBA Emerging Leaders Initiative, a federal training initiative that specifically focuses on executives of businesses poised for growth in historically challenged communities. The initiative provides these executives with the organizational framework, resource network, and motivation required to build sustainable businesses and promote economic development within urban communities. To date, the Emerging Leaders Initiative has aided nearly 1,300 urban and Native American small business owners in sustaining and growing their businesses. Participants have accessed more than $26 million in new financing since graduating the program. They have also secured federal, state, local, and tribal contracts with a cumulative total of $330 million. It's a true success story for small businesses.

Small businesses are you and me. They are our neighbors and friends. They are the heart and soul of this nation. Many continue to be spawned by immigrants who create jobs and prosperity for other Americans.

five

PASSING THE BATON OF THE DREAM: EDUCATION AS THE CONDUIT

Being the children of immigrants is not easy. When Maggie and I had our three children, we were just getting our feet on the ground. Our command of English was shaky, and in our household, where my mother also lived with us, Chinese was the first language our children spoke. In our small community in Florida, we didn't know other Asians. There wasn't a thriving Chinese community like those that existed in New York City or San Francisco. Our children had American names, but in their early years, they felt different. My daughter Jessica still remembers her first day of preschool, being unable to speak or understand English. When all the children rose to recite the Pledge of Allegiance, she "freaked out" and wanted to go home.

Looking back, Jessica admits, "There were times I didn't understand why I was different, why I looked different, why I wasn't like the other kids." But with time and effort, we put those fears to rest.

We worked hard to give them a vision of what they could be. They were born in America, and Maggie would tell them—not just our son but also our daughters—"You can be president one day."

Today, they are successful adults—highly educated entrepreneurs in business, engineering, and computer science. They all love America and are committed to making a meaningful contribution. How did they get there?

In our household, the path was very simple. We understood that while America was a place of opportunity, you had to make it happen and work hard for it. There was no easy way. Early on, as I worked long hours to build a business, Maggie took over our children's education. She had a strong belief that what they learned at school was not enough.

When our kids started school, we were surprised by the schedule. In Taiwan, we began the school day at 8:00 in the morning and didn't get out until 5 p.m. If a big test was coming up, we might stay until 7:00 or 8:00 in the evening. In Florida, the school day ended at 2:00 in the afternoon.

Maggie thought our children needed more. So, while their friends were outside playing, our children were seated at the dining room table, studying, memorizing maps of the world, copying passages from the encyclopedia— whatever Maggie could think of to give them an edge and the discipline of study. She gave them incentives and rewards for getting straight As—which they all did. "You must push your minds," she would tell them.

Maggie believed that excelling in math was key. She'd give the kids 10 problems. If they got one wrong, she'd give them 10 more. Two wrong, she'd give them 20 more. She'd take out the encyclopedia and tell them to pick a state to learn about. They memorized the details of every state—right down to the state bird. It may not have been crucial information, but the point was to help them develop study skills.

Maggie also got involved with the schools, helping to start programs that would increase their knowledge and cultural awareness. She was not a so-called tiger mom, but she took her role seriously. In Maggie's view, the home was the place where success was molded. She did not believe in abdicating that responsibility to the schools.

This educational work ethic is common to Asian immigrants, and it pays off. Claudia Kolker, who wrote the book *The Immigrant Advantage: What We Can Learn from Newcomers to America about Health, Happiness, and Hope*, calls it "preemptive tutoring." Usually, when kids have tutors, it's because they are failing a subject. Preemptive tutoring is different. "It's to get ahead, to always be a step ahead," Kolker says.

I asked my daughters recently whether they ever resented how much harder they had to work than their friends. "We knew you came to America for us—to make our lives better," Jessica told me. "You moved from a country where you knew people and could speak the language to a country where you didn't know people and had to learn a new language. We wanted to work hard because you worked hard. We knew it would make our future better." And it has.

HELPING THE NEXT GENERATION succeed is a real passion of mine. I think in many ways we've got it all wrong in how we prepare young people for the workforce. We say we want them to succeed, and then we pour hundreds of thousands of dollars into liberal arts education and they can't get jobs. I'll admit that I was pretty firm with my kids. I wanted them to be engineers because I knew they could get jobs or become entrepreneurs. Jessica and John both became engineers. My youngest daughter, Jennifer, balked. She wasn't interested in engineering. She announced to me that she wanted to pursue a double major in neuroscience and behavioral psychology and business. It was ambitious, but I didn't see the benefit right away because of my engineering bias. I responded, "Your major is like studying flower arranging." I was wrong, of course. Jennifer excelled, and she's already started three companies, so my preference for engineering was a bit too rigid. Even so, the point is still the same. It drives me crazy the way career counselors are failing our children. They tell them, "Follow your dreams." I think that's wrong. If a young person has a dream of becoming a painter, there's nothing wrong with that. But he or she needs to have an expanded vision. Counselors have to encourage kids to look at the whole picture—not just follow their dreams but also be practical. If you're liberal arts major, it's going to be difficult for you after you graduate, no matter how you look at it.

I sometimes counsel young people, and I push them hard to make a connection between education and work. Recently, I asked a student about his aspirations. "I love music," he said. "When I play the guitar, I am transported out of this world."

"That's great," I said. "I like your enthusiasm. The problem is can you make a living playing guitar?" Obviously, there are people making a living from music. I don't denigrate that. The question I was asking was could *he* make a living playing music?

It's been my observation—and this is backed up by many studies—that musical ability and computer ability go hand in hand. So I told him, "Why don't you study computer science and play music on the side? Maximize your creativity and your job prospects all at the same time."

It's our obligation to lead young people on a path that will help them succeed. We have to change our thinking. The old thinking was that college is a meaningful experience, no matter what you studied. I believe that's no longer true—and a lot of experts are starting to come around to that way of thinking. The Georgetown University Center on Education and the Workforce wrote a report called "Hard Times: College Majors, Unemployment, and Earnings—Not All College Degrees Are Created Equal." The report put it bluntly: "The risk of unemployment among recent college graduates depends on their major."

For example, the unemployment rate for graduates with fine arts degrees is 12.6 percent, while engineering graduates have an unemployment rate of only 4.9 percent. Anthropology graduates have a 10.5 percent unemployment rate, while nursing graduates have a 4 percent unemployment rate.

For some, vocational schools are the answer. Enrollment is booming at schools that teach "hard" skills because students are more focused than ever on their job prospects. It used to be that kids would say, "I don't know what I want to be, and college is a place to find myself." They don't have that luxury anymore. With that attitude, they're more likely to find themselves in the unemployment line. College is no longer a sure path to success.

In addition to fields of study, we also need to teach kids the real-world skills they'll need to succeed. It's not enough to know how to write computer code. You need to know how to think creatively and work with others. You can be a genius, but if you can't sit across a table and communicate your ideas in an appealing way, it means nothing. I'm a good example of that. When you look at my career path, notice how many times I survived by communicating well or by being likable. We don't teach communication skills in school, so even the most adept engineering school graduates can fail because they lack the language of human relationships. Business is defined by relationships. You have to make people want to work with you and want to help you do well.

When we hire young engineers to work in our company, we are not just looking for people who graduated at the top of their class. We want to know that they have good social skills, that they can think outside of the box, that they're excited about creating, that they have a strong work ethic. For us, the "right" people see themselves as lifelong learners whose education doesn't end when they throw their caps in the air.

Richard Murnane, an economist with the Harvard School of Education, conducted a study on the relationship between cognitive and noncognitive skills and future earnings. The noncognitive skills assessed were:

- Willingness to assume responsibility

- Independence

- Outgoing character

- Persistence

- Emotional stability

- Initiative

- Social skills

Murnane and his researchers found that noncognitive skills were stronger predictors of wages, employment status, and annual earnings than were cognitive skills. In a presentation to a National Research Council conference assessing twenty-first-century skills, he added that the importance of noncognitive skills wasn't just limited to a narrow review of jobs, salaries, and promotions. These skills are the building blocks of being good human beings and good citizens—for "leading a contributing life in a pluralistic democracy."

Murnane spoke of the complex problems America faces and how solving them depends on a population that knows how to think and knows how to relate to others. He's absolutely right. Preparing our kids for success means much more than preparing them for jobs. To take advantage of America's promise of "life, liberty, and the pursuit of happiness," they must also be "complete" human beings.

The Consortium for Entrepreneurship is an organization that encourages young people to be successful by promoting education in entrepreneurship. It points out that entrepreneurs aren't born—they become that way by harnessing the experiences of their lives and learning how. While there is no degree in entrepreneurship, they get that way by developing good support skills including communications, interpersonal abilities, economic understanding, digital skills, marketing, management, and math/finance skills. According to the consortium, these skills must be developed in young people so they can be poised to realize their full promise.

IN RECENT YEARS we've heard a lot about the technology gap in American universities. That is, not enough students are pursuing studies—and eventually careers—in the science and technology fields. Increasingly, immigrants are filling the gap. According to the National Venture Capital Association, when companies recruit on U.S. college campuses, they find that a large percentage of graduate students in important technology fields are foreign nationals. Just look at the numbers. In 2011, more than 65 percent of students receiving a PhD and 60 percent of students receiving a master's degree in electrical engineering were foreign nationals. Furthermore, in virtually every technical field, international students achieved 50 percent or more of the degrees.

The question is, what do these foreign students know about making it in America that homegrown students may not know? Economists and educators have expressed alarm that American students are not pursuing STEM (science, technology, engineering, and mathematics) degrees at a fast enough pace to fill all the highly skilled jobs that are available. According to a government study, the United States needs 400,000 new graduates in all STEM fields by 2015 to fill the need. But while the technology sector has grown at four times the rate of other fields, student enrollment is not keeping pace. Only about 15 percent of all college graduates have STEM majors or minors.

The real-world implications are astounding. Between 2011 and 2015, an estimated 1.7 million jobs will be created in cloud computing in North America—including mobile application ("apps") technology, which has created 311,000 jobs in the "app economy." By 2018, the bulk of STEM jobs will be in computing—71 percent. Who will fill these jobs, and why aren't students rushing to grab the brass ring of future prosperity?

Unfortunately, STEM education still gets a bad rap. There is a general belief that these fields are too hard and the studies are boring. Most American students resist what they consider a depressing and difficult course of study.

In my opinion, a large share of the responsibility—and perhaps the blame—goes to high school and college career counselors. Think of it. We do not call them *dream* counselors. We do not call them *wish* counselors. We do not even call them *study* counselors. We call them *career* counselors. Their responsibility is to lead students into fields that promise fulfilling and productive careers. But too often they fall down on the job. For example, they make rigid assumptions about students' prospects, sending the math and science "stars" into science and engineering and the arts and literature "stars" into liberal arts. Or they offer only lackluster counseling about college and community college opportunities.

A national survey conducted by the Public Agenda Research Company and funded by the Bill and Melinda Gates Foundation highlighted the troubling state of high school counseling. The report, titled "'Can I Get a Little Advice?' How an Overstretched High School Guidance System Is Undermining Students' College Aspirations," asked people in their 20s who'd had at least some college to rate the effectiveness of their high school counselors. Nearly two-thirds said the counselors had done a "fair" or "poor" job of helping them select the right college or career. Fifty percent said they felt like "another face in the crowd."

A big part of the problem is lack of counseling resources. Although professional groups such as the American School Counselor Association say that a student-counselor ratio of 250 students to one counselor is optimal, this is far from the typical state of affairs in most public schools. In California, the ratio is closer to 1,000 students for every one counselor available. In Arizona, Minnesota, Utah, and the District of Columbia, the ratio is typically more than 700 to one. The national average is 460 to one.

But the news isn't all bad. Increasingly, states and universities are getting into the act to help students in the lower grades prepare for their futures.

One such program is the state of Massachusetts' Connecting Activities, a state-funded Department of Elementary and Secondary Education–led initiative designed to drive and sustain the school-to-career system across the Commonwealth. The program supplies participating schools with employer outreach specialists, who work in close coordination with local chambers of commerce and career centers to provide workplace experiences, mentoring, and training to high school students. For example, at Natick High School, the Connecting Activities Career Specialist worked with the guidance department to provide college and career readiness opportunities for juniors and seniors, including job shadows at local companies, college and career speakers, and internships. This is just one example of many initiatives that are being led by state governments across the nation.

New York has recently launched a statewide school-to-career program that will interface with high schools and community colleges, and member schools and students will receive accelerated job training. The program is supported by GlobalFoundries, Cisco, GE Healthcare, Wegmans supermarkets, and Lockheed Martin. According to one corporate sponsor, graduating students will be first in line for jobs at companies such as IBM, starting at competitive salaries.

In Marin County, California, the Marin County School to Career Partnership brings together schools, businesses, and organizations to create exciting educational opportunities for students. The partnership is a project of the Marin County Office of Education working on behalf of the school districts in the community. The partnership serves students from diverse academic, social, and economic backgrounds. On-the-job experiences allow students to explore potential careers, think about their future educational goals, and develop skills necessary for success in the workplace. The partnership collaborates with more than 200 businesses and organizations, providing learning experiences for the students of today while they are developing their skilled workforce of tomorrow. More than 100 local businesses, representing virtually all fields, have signed up to offer internships as part of the program.

The Department of Education is committed to supporting changes in schools that will enhance career readiness. A 2013 initiative designed to better prepare students for the demands of a high-tech economy will reward schools that develop partnerships with employers and create classes that focus on STEM skills. The department acknowledges that many of America's international competitors offer students a more rigorous and relevant education in their middle and high school years, and the United States must do more.

The initiative includes a $300-million commitment to a competitive grant program that supports partnerships between school districts; institutions of higher education; and business, industry, nonprofits, and community-based organizations to redesign high schools. Redesigned high schools will put in place learning models that allow students to graduate from high school with college credit and career-related experience. The department will also put more money into the execution of the 2006 Carl D. Perkins Vocational and Technical Education Act, which increased focus on the academic achievement of career and technical education students.

These programs and others demonstrate a promising commitment across the nation to strengthening school-to-career efforts. There is a renewed realization that education has to be infused with purpose—and that purpose is to prepare our young people to work and thrive in the economy.

The business community can play an active part in offering real-world business education, through internships and by volunteering in the schools. Another impressive initiative in this realm is a collaboration between Corporate Voices for Working Families and the American Association of School Administrators (AASA). These partners are working together to help communities build broader relationships between business and education to better ensure that students graduate high school equipped with the skills necessary to thrive in the workplace and in life. Their goal is to implement Ready by 21, a design for improving achievement goals by 2021. Daniel Domenich, the AASA executive director, points out, "The fact of the matter is that this requires a community effort. Not just the school's effort, not the YMCA's effort, not the United Way's effort, not the businesses' and corporations' effort. A joint effort that everybody agrees on is necessary for success." That's a goal we all can share.

I've provided internships to many kids—including my own—through my businesses. Every summer, we offer a few jobs for local kids, but we also have between 10 and 15 internships where we're really dedicated to teaching them the ropes. They move from department to department and get two weeks of experience in every arena. In this way, students may find that they are better suited to one area than another or enjoy one more than another. It's also the best way for them to learn how a company functions.

It can be a little tricky sometimes because as a defense company, we have many classified functions. But I insist on intern programs, so we work around it.

In 2001, Joel Szabat, a California public servant and son of an immigrant, founded the International Leadership Foundation (ILF) with a goal of giving scholarships and encouraging young Asian Americans to become leaders. Joel, who is currently deputy assistant secretary for transportation policy, feels strongly that we have an obligation to enable the next generation of leaders. When I first heard about Joel's organization, I was immediately excited. These were ideals we shared. I'm proud to serve as chairman of ILF, which has thrived in the decade since its inception. I work very closely with Joel's wife, Chiling Tong, who is the chief executive officer and founding president. Chiling is a remarkable woman with extensive experience in domestic and international economic and business development and has received several prestigious awards for her work with small minority business enterprises.

One of ILF's signature programs provides 30 to 40 two-month positions in the government for Asian American youngsters. My daughter Jennifer got into one of the programs, working in the Department of Commerce. That's when she fell in love with Washington, D.C.

Another great ILF program is the Young Ambassador Program, which hosts 60 outstanding students from Asia to participate in a unique 12-day program in Washington, D.C., and the northeast region. Again, the goal is to prepare the next generation of international young leaders to address the global business and political issues in our changing world. The international experience involves an exciting series of lectures, excursions, and discussions on topics ranging from international business relations to public policy and the legislative process. Excursions include visits to the White House, Congress, federal agencies, the United Nations, Wall Street, and top U.S. universities. I am confident that these students leave the program poised to be leaders in whatever they do.

I'm proud to be the chairman of this organization. I see it bearing fruit every year with each new crop of remarkable students. But I also believe we must reach out to all young people—not just the top students, not just the so-called best and brightest.

After World War II, the GI Bill made college accessible for millions of veterans, and it has often been cited as the key to building the middle class in the decades after the war. Today is different. A four-year college education isn't necessarily the road to the middle class for everyone. I believe that community colleges get undersold when they are clearly a better option for some students and sometimes they are even the gateway to better careers. College Measures analyzed data from three states and found that not only did new graduates of technical or occupational programs out-earn their community college peers in nontechnical programs but also they out-earned bachelor's degree holders. In addition, a two-year course is just a better fit for some students. It's more affordable, and it gives them a chance to figure out their strengths and interests before investing in an expensive course of study that might not suit them.

WHEN I LOOK BACK at my own formative school years, I recall what a poor student I was—bored and disinterested in the classroom. I saw myself as a free spirit, whatever that meant. That attitude didn't serve me well, and I wonder how different my experience would have been if I'd had visionary teachers. We must always keep in mind that our youth, our most precious resource, don't just grow on their own initiative like sturdy oaks in a forest. They need proper cultivation. I think it's true that there are no bad kids. There are only bad advisors.

I always tell young people that their possibilities are unlimited. It is up to them to figure out what they want to do and how hard they're willing to work to do it. Nobody else will decide their future. If they're disgruntled and feel dismayed about their chances, I give them my mother's advice. She used to tell me, "If the pond is too small for a big fish, you need to find a bigger pond."

HOW AMERICA IS STILL THE INNOVATION NATION

often hear people complaining that America's manufacturing base, which has been the bedrock of our nation's prosperity, is dying and permanently putting an end to millions of jobs. Factories are shutting down, and jobs are being outsourced, never to return. Many are depressed about that. But I see it another way. The notion of lost opportunity could mean a lack of imagination.

Opportunity isn't the domain of one industry or another. It's about recognizing a need. I believe that if we can catch every opportunity, identify every need in this country, and figure out solutions to those needs, we could probably create 20,000 new companies a year. In other words, if we think of ourselves as problem solvers, we will succeed.

Looking around, we see that some old corporations saved themselves by reinvention. In his book, *Who Says Elephants Can't Dance? Leading a Great Enterprise through Dramatic Change*, Lou Gerstner writes about turning around IBM. In the early 1990s, IBM was a lumbering giant that wasn't keeping pace with the new, more nimble technology companies. So it dared to completely change its model. As Gerstner put it, "Who says elephants can't dance?" IBM showed that even the largest companies can change. But the best new companies and individuals who lead them are those that incorporate change into their fundamental model. Apple is probably the best example of that. It started out building desktop computers, but its business model is to keep recognizing new needs and meeting them. No one thinks of Apple as just a computer company anymore.

Some of America's most iconic companies are struggling for survival, and the key will be their ability to recognize and grab new opportunities—because if they don't, others will. These include some of the biggest and brightest, such as McDonald's and Ford Motor Company. A few years back, everyone thought America's auto industry was dead. But then Ford brought in Alan Mulally—not a "car guy" but an airline industry executive—and he turned the company around. He could shake things up because he wasn't stuck in conventional thinking.

SINCE ITS INCEPTION, America has self-identified as a nation based on innovation. Our system of government was the first innovation. The greatest inventions of our times emerged from this spirit of opportunity. America launched the era of telecommunications, changed the face of mortality with penicillin, led the industrial revolution, and produced great innovators such as Thomas Edison and Henry Ford. There is no question that innovation made America great and made the world a better place as a result. But in recent years, with the decline of the manufacturing sector, we have experienced a challenge to our identity as an innovation nation.

A few years ago, John Kao, an organizational and innovation advisor (and first-generation Chinese American), wrote a controversial book titled *Innovation Nation: How America Is Losing Its Innovation Edge,*

Why It Matters, and What We Can Do to Get It Back. Kao's premise was that America had grown complacent in its dominance, while other nations—from China to Hungary—were fired up. "It is a crucial moment in time," he wrote, "a historic tipping point perhaps. Just as we are beginning to slack off, others are stepping on the gas." His book was a passionate cry for more investment in innovation: "What is required is nothing less than a major commitment of America's resources, human and financial, to rejuvenate our innovation engine."

Yanzhong Huang, a senior fellow for global health at the Council on Foreign Relations, blogging on *Asia Unbound*, in October 2013, writes that America is in danger of being sapped of its innovative power. As an example, he points to funding trends in the National Institutes of Health, which is the source of much scientific ingenuity. He points out that between 2003 and 2013, the number of applications increased from nearly 35,000 to more than 51,000, while NIH appropriations shrunk from $21 billion to $16 billion (in 1995 dollars). As a consequence, it has become increasingly difficult for our scientists to garner an NIH grant. Overall application success rates fell from 32 percent in 2000 to 18 percent in 2012. Comparing this trend to that in China, Huang points out that the investment is only expanding there, where government research funding has been growing at a rate of 20 percent. Huang urges America to restore its bold, can-do principles; to avoid government gridlock (which led to the devastating government shutdown); and to remember what we're all about.

Writing in *Forbes*, retired Lockheed Martin Chairman and CEO Norm Augustine presents a rallying cry for renewed innovation: "Global leadership is not a birthright. Despite what many Americans believe, our nation does not possess an innate knack for greatness. Greatness must be worked for and won by each new generation. Right now that is not happening. But we still have time. If we place the emphasis we should on education, research and innovation we can lead the world in the decades to come."

The bottom line is that no other country in the world can compete with an America that remains true to its principles. Those principles are expressed not only in ideology but also in tactics. Innovation happens on the ground, in thousands of individual situations when a spark is lit.

AS MY COMPANY GREW, I became increasingly committed to innovation. I was always looking for new opportunities. One day, I got a call from a guy named Marty Skalka, who owned a company called Computer Science Inc. I didn't know Marty that well; we occasionally saw each other at local meetings, but we weren't close friends. I knew that CSI worked with some government contracts, but even before Marty reached out, I'd heard that there were some financial problems that were making it hard for him to deliver on his government contracts.

When Marty called me, he sounded resigned to the failure of his business. "Paul, I'm going to file Chapter 11 in two weeks," he said. "But there's one piece of the business I'm not willing to see go down the drain with the rest of the company. I'm an old guy in my 70s, but you're young and energetic. Why don't you look at it? Maybe you can take it over. What do you say?"

I was pretty surprised to get this call. "Marty," I said, "I can't just blindly take over your business. I appreciate the offer, but I need to know whether it fits in with our core competencies. If it's something that's not electronics related, I don't think I can handle it."

He got that, but he assured me that this business, called ActiGraph, was right up my alley. ActiGraph produced wearable electronic monitors for the army called accelerometers that calculated energy expenditures and calorie needs. It helped the army decide troop movements, meal plans, and other logistics.

My interest was piqued. "Oh," I said, "that's very interesting."

He jumped on my interest. "So, just take it. It's yours."

"Marty," I laughed. "I have to pay you."

"Fine, fine," he said. "Just pay for my inventory. Say, about $20,000. And I'd like you to hire three of my assemblers."

"Well, I guess that sounds fair," I said, "but as a defense company, I can't just write somebody a check. I have to have a record. If I want to pay you $5, I have to show the government why I paid you the $5. That's the rule. I'll send some people over to check the inventory."

So I sent Keith and an engineer, and they analyzed Marty's inventory. We also interviewed the three employees that Marty wanted us to hire, and we were glad to hire them. They used to work for Harris, and Keith and I knew them very well.

When we were done running the numbers, I called Marty. "I don't think I can pay you $20,000," I said.

"Oh, OK," he said quickly, "whatever you can pay. You're taking my three guys. That's enough."

"You don't understand," I told him. "Marty, your inventory is worth $70,000. I have to pay you $70,000."

"Wow. Are you sure?"

"Well, that's what the inventory shows," I assured him.

It meant a lot to me to give Marty value for his company. The inventory might not have been worth $70,000—maybe closer to $50,000 or $60,000. But I figured the guy was down, and I wasn't going to kick him. I didn't know then just how big ActiGraph would become, but I saw something there, a spark of potential that I wanted to follow. One key principle of growth is to spot those sparks, even when they're tiny, and nurture them and see where you can take them.

I asked Jeff Arnett, who was at Total Parts Plus, to run the new company. His background was computer science and sales. Jeff's a gung-ho guy, and he was willing to jump in with both feet. I explained my philosophy, which was to take it slow and build step-by-step. The very first thing we needed to do was to go to the existing customers. There were only a handful of them. We needed to find out how they used the technology, what was good about it, where the kinks were, and who else would benefit from the product. We had to find a growth market. I approached ActiGraph the way I'd approached my other businesses: find out what the customers needed, grow from the base, and do it the old-fashioned way—with lots of elbow grease. In the process, we found our niche. It revealed itself to us like a glowing light.

The facts are that some of the most expensive costs for any government around the world involve health care, newer generations are less healthy than previous generations, and childhood obesity is escalating. Observing the trends, we devised an innovative new direction for ActiGraph.

We soon realized that we held in our hands a powerful tool that could help find solutions to monitoring overall well-being, not just for members of the military but also for the entire population. ActiGraph's mission became to improve world health by providing the most accurate and scientifically validated activity and sleep-monitoring hardware and software solutions to leading research, pharmaceutical, healthcare, and wellness organizations.

In the coming years, ActiGraph grew as we offered essential tools to the healthcare industry. For example, ActiGraph devices were used to collect physical activity data on approximately 15,000 subjects aged six years and older in the National Health and Nutrition Examination Survey, an ongoing program of studies conducted by the National Center for Health Statistics assessing the health and nutritional status of adults and children in the United States.

Childhood obesity is a critical issue. ActiGraph devices are used to measure physical activity of parents, young children, and adolescents, with a total sample size of approximately 2,800 participants in the Childhood Obesity Prevention and Treatment Research (COPTR) program, one of the first long-term obesity prevention and treatment research studies in children.

In a large-scale European study investigating the different factors influencing obesity and related disorders in children aged two to nine in 11 European countries, ActiGraph activity monitors were used to collect physical activity and combined physical activity and heart rate data on a subsample of approximately 7,500 participants.

We also got involved with the landmark study conducted by Brigham and Women's Hospital and Harvard Medical School that began in 1993 as a randomized trial of low-dose aspirin and vitamin E supplementation for cardiovascular disease and cancer prevention in nearly 40,000 female health professionals aged 45 and older. The trial concluded in 2004, and the Women's Health Study has now evolved into one of the largest and longest-running observational studies of women's health in the United States. An ancillary study examining physical activity and health outcomes is currently under way, involving approximately 30,000 women from the original trial. ActiGraph devices are being used to objectively measure physical activity in study participants.

These and other projects allowed ActiGraph to gain credibility in the healthcare research arena. Today, we have a robust package for researchers. This success opened the way for us to get involved with pharmaceutical drug trials, which we think will be our largest business segment.

As we grew, we put together a scientific advisory board and a software advisory panel to find out how we could stay ahead of competition. What is the next area? And how do we keep engineering our products so they are better and expand their range?

In 2012, ActiGraph won the National Institutes of Health exclusive contract. NIH is the largest medical institution of the U.S. government in Washington, D.C. Now, every time NIH does a sleep disorder, obesity, or cancer rehabilitation study, they use ActiGraph. This contract extends to countries around the world. It's a big opportunity for us. We really have to be on our toes.

Innovation is a constant. We operate from a standard of continuous improvement. The ActiGraph of today is nothing like Marty's original company. In the past seven years or so, we have reengineered the product four or five times. That's how you're always ahead of your competitors, and that's why we can sell ActiGraph for $300 or $400, more than similar products. Reputation and excellence are worth something.

ActiGraph has become a gem in Pensacola. There isn't an engineer within a hundred miles who doesn't want to work in this innovative environment. If you visit ActiGraph, it might remind you of a Silicon Valley–style operation. It's buzzing with creativity and dog friendly, and there's a game room for our young engineers to blow off steam. The feeling is very entrepreneurial. New ideas and breakthroughs are encouraged. No one's crucified for making a mistake. It's all part of the process. Our employees know that not only are they responding to interesting technical and technological challenges but also they're making a difference that could positively affect millions of people. That's very gratifying.

ONE SELDOM-ACKNOWLEDGED characteristic of American immigrants is the ability to connect globally—to take newly discovered opportunities and spread them around the world. Immigrants have a deeper understanding of the connectedness of the globe and often have the connections and resources to make things happen. We live in a global economy, and we share the environment. The actions of one nation have consequences for others.

Living in the United States, I became even more aware of the need for clean energy solutions, especially in my birthplace. On my many visits to China, I have always been disturbed by the unfathomable level of pollution. Returning home, I would usually have a bad cough for weeks.

I wanted to do something about it and to make a contribution that would have global ramifications. Fortunately, I was able to turn my sense of global responsibility into action when I was invited to join the Harvard University Asia Center as a senior research fellow on energy efficiency.

Research and study revealed that the problem was coal. The United States and China are the two largest coal-producing countries in the world. It's the cheapest and most accessible source of fuel. In the United States, we're experimenting with many alternative technologies, but this has not been the case in China because of coal's ubiquity and affordability. There are more than half a million coal-burning factories in China. The government is concerned about pollution and openly committed to reducing it, but it can't ask half a million factories to stop burning coal. There's literally nothing it can do about it. So, I was very interested in figuring out a solution that would keep the coal but decrease its pollutants. That's the challenge that kept me awake at night and excited me with its potential.

To work on that project, I founded Ecotech Global Solutions, an energy management company, along with my partners, the China Quality Certification Center and Zhejiang University. We invented a piece of equipment that would make coal burning more efficient. Our first target for testing it was the ceramics industry, which is pervasive in China and is one of the worst polluters. It's a very low-tech industry and incredibly cheap to run. Basically, you just take clay and burn it. It's extremely dirty.

The function of our machine was first to pulverize the coal and make it into a powder and then to create oxygen to blow the coal into the burning chamber, thereby increasing the temperature. Once you increase the temperature, you don't have to burn as much coal. The concept is actually very simple.

Once we built the unit and obtained permission to test it in a factory, things got interesting. Like every new technology, there were kinks to work out. It didn't operate smoothly at first. I spent a couple weeks in a factory while trying to solve the problem, and at the end of every day, I was black with soot and coughing from the coal dust. But we figured it out, and that was a very happy day for me.

The possibilities are unbelievable. I predict that our units could mean reducing the amount of pollution in China by 20 percent. Imagine that! And the benefit isn't only for China because, remember, we live in an interconnected world. The air pollution in Beijing has already reached Alaska and California. So, in this case, what's good for the world is very good for America. Being an innovator means having a big idea and the will to carry it out.

HOW DO YOU MAKE sure you do business with an innovation mindset? These are the eight principles I adopted early on in my life, and they've stood the test of time:

1. Never say no before you say maybe.

When you say no, it closes the door. It turns off the opportunity. I can think of a dozen times in my life when I could have said no but I paused and said instead, "Let me think about it. Let me investigate it." When Marty approached me about taking over ActiGraph, it would have been easy for me to pass. I wasn't looking for a new company, especially in a field I didn't know a lot about. But I took a small step forward. I agreed to listen. And the rest is history.

2. Stay curious.

I was blessed with a curious mind. I really want to know how things work. I'm a tinkerer at heart. Albert Einstein talked about a "holy curiosity." I like that image. Curiosity is what took us into space. I believe that we're all on earth to engage in a process of lifetime learning. Knowledge doesn't end at the university door. It's not a finite thing. Looking back, I can say that

I learned most of what I know about business by living it and by always pushing myself to learn and grow. When I started Ecotech, Maggie asked me, "Why are you doing this? When are you going to slow down?" I told her it was because I found the problem interesting. It energized me. As for slowing down, maybe never.

3. Be bold.

After my son, John, graduated from college, he struggled to find a job that he loved. As an engineer, it might have been easy, but he was determined to get into the gaming business, which was his passion. I was skeptical because I knew little about that specific field. I thought maybe it was frivolous. But John was determined. He was living with us while he looked for work, and one day he told me, "There's a company in New York City that produces my favorite game. If I could work for that company, I'd be so happy." But he had no idea how to get his foot in the door. I urged him to take a bold chance. He had a contact name, so I suggested, "Why don't you let him know that over Christmas you'll be in New York for a couple of weeks and you'd like to talk to him just for a few minutes? Put yourself there, and give him the opening." John looked at me doubtfully. "Are you sure?" he asked. "I'm sure," I said. "All it will cost him is a few minutes of time. He doesn't have to fly you in or put you up." He did it and got the job. All it took was initiative and the willingness to be bold. There's nothing to lose by taking a chance, believing in yourself, and doing what it takes to let people know about you.

4. Strive to understand what makes people tick.

Those of us in technical and technological fields can sometimes forget that what we do is really about serving people. If you keep that principle at the forefront of your mind, you will be innovation oriented. That's because people have an endless number of wants and needs and the innovative thinker is going to want to come up with solutions. Understanding customers is much more important than spending money. Year after year, the Booz & Company Global Innovation 1000 study reinforces the fact that there is no correlation between the amount of money that companies spend on research and development and their overall financial performance. However, the top innovators generate ideas from the most old-fashioned method in the world—direct customer observation and feedback.

5. Build relationships.

For me, the relationships I build are even more important than the products I create. Time and again, supportive hands have reached out to me, and I've done the same for others. You lose nothing by opening yourself to others and developing trust. I've also learned within my own companies that when I treat employees with respect—as partners in prosperity, not worker drones—I get back what I give a hundredfold in creativity and effort. When workers are invested both physically and emotionally, there's nothing they can't achieve. I always say, share the pain, but share the gain, too.

One of my models is Lee Iacocca. I still admire the way he turned Chrysler around when it was on the brink of bankruptcy in the 1980s. But one thing in particular impressed me. During Chrysler's hardest times, Iacocca announced that he would take only $1 for a salary. He felt it was his obligation to share the pain. This was very inspirational for the workers. They trusted him more because he was in the trenches with them.

6. Build wisely.

Innovation is a process, not a destination. I've always built my companies slowly and was never in a rush to get big. Often when I talk to students or young engineers, they have stars in their eyes. They've heard stories about people making $50 million just by inventing an app. They're restless to get moving and make a bundle. In my own companies, I've had executives who wanted to move fast, to take on more projects. But I had a firm principle of never moving beyond what I knew we could produce. It's tempting when people wave money in front of your eyes, but it's not a good strategy for long-term growth.

7. Welcome new ideas, even from unlikely sources.

Ideas are the engine of innovation. You can't be an innovator if you're a know-it-all. Listen—really listen—to what others have to say. Hold open meetings with your employees and kick around ideas. Google began as a great model of this principle. One day a week, employees were allowed to work on their own projects. Not only did this practice foster independence and creativity but also it allowed employees to drive innovation. According to Google, the practice was responsible for 50 percent of its big ideas, including Gmail. Unfortunately, Google discontinued the program, but other innovative companies, inspired by the idea, started their own similar programs—including LinkedIn's InCubator, which allows engineers time to work on original product ideas, and Apple's Blue Sky, which allows some workers to spend several weeks on their own projects.

8. Adhere to strong values.

When we talk about the "culture" of a company, we are really talking about its values. Your values are everything; they're the heart of your business. A value-driven company doesn't cut corners: it behaves in a trustworthy manner with customers, competitors, and employees; it is a responsible partner in the community; and it has a human core—that is, it's not just about money.

Innovation is so important, so fundamental to the American spirit, that it may stand alone as our core principle for greatness. "Do you know what my favorite renewable fuel is?" asks Thomas Friedman. "An ecosystem for innovation." I couldn't have said it better.

Aerial view of Ellis Island with Statue of Liberty, New York City.

CREDIT; iofoto / Shutterstock.

Vintage photo c. 1907, immigrants disembarking from a ship at Ellis Island in New York.

CREDIT; © Archives Pics / Alamy.

Immigrants awaiting examination at Ellis Island, c. 1902.

Processing of immigrants, Ellis Island, New York City.

CREDIT; © Ewing Galloway / UIG / age fotostock.

A Chinese grocery in San Francisco, c. 1890s.

Albertype reproduction of a photograph.

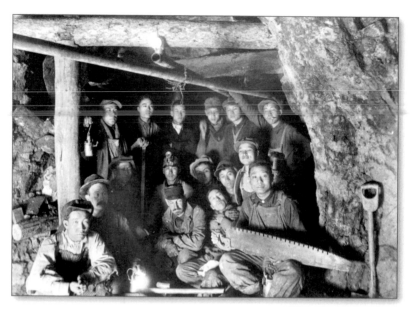

Chinese miners, Idaho Springs, c. 1920–1930.

CREDIT; American Photographer (20th century) / Denver Public Library, Western History Collection / The Bridgeman Art Library.

Track layers gang building the Union Pacific Railroad through American wilderness, c. 1860s.

CREDIT; American Photographer (19th century) / Private Collection / Peter Newark American Pictures / The Bridgeman Art Library.

Two builders during the construction of the Empire State
Building, c. 1933.

CREDIT; Science and Society / SuperStock.

Men and women working on a radio assembly line in the Washington,
DC, area, c. 1925.

CREDIT; © Courtesy: Everett Collection / age fotostock.

Mott Street in New York City's Chinatown c. 1900 presents a cosmopolitan scene mixing Asian and American-European dress and faces. The street is lined with restaurants, laundries, and pushcarts.

CREDIT© Courtesy: Everett Collection / age fotostock.

Agricultural workers, possibly Japanese-Americans, harvesting pineapples on a plantation in Hawaii, c. 1920. Japanese-Americans started immigrating to Hawaii and the American West Coast in 1885 after the U.S. exclusion of Chinese immigrants.

New York, New York: c. 1926. A little boy shows his patriotism for his new country as he arrives at Ellis Island, the gateway to America, in New York Harbor. After long journeys, most people are very happy to finally land at Ellis Island.

New York, New York: December 4, 2009. Miled Manzur (L), of the Dominican Republic and a member of the U.S. Army, Marianne Pilgrim of Canada, and Yong Shin from Korea, also with the army, wave flags during their naturalization ceremony held in the Great Hall on Ellis Island. More than 100 people from 44 countries were sworn in as American citizens during the ceremony.

CREDIT; © Monika Graff / The Image Works.

seven

THE SECRET TO THE ENTREPRENEURIAL SPIRIT

My daughters, Jessica and Jennifer, caught the entrepreneurial bug early. In the fifth grade, Jennifer made a video documentary called "Land of Opportunity" that featured my story of emigrating from Taiwan and becoming a successful entrepreneur. Naturally, I was very proud of her.

They hadn't been out of school that long when they decided to start their own company. I didn't try to dissuade them. In fact, I was very, very excited. I thought their decision to become entrepreneurs was the best thing that ever happened to them—and to me too. I felt that they finally got some DNA out of me.

It was risky, but I believed—and I told them—that if they didn't try, they'd never know what was possible. As I said at the time, getting out of your comfort zone, jumping into the water—that's a good thing, even if the water is cold and the wind is blowing. And that's what they did. They had a big idea and wanted to make it fly.

By way of context, let me say that all my kids loved video games. In fact, my son, John, has made game programming his career. When they were kids, we were pretty strict about it. They weren't allowed to watch TV or play video games Monday through Thursday, and Sunday was Chinese school, so they had a window from Friday after school to Saturday night, and during that time they played video games like crazy.

When they were thinking about creating a product in 2007, Jessica and Jennifer thought back to how engaged they were with gaming, and they saw a way to combine that sense of engagement with education.

At the time, they noticed some very troubling statistics about the public schools in Washington, D.C. Overall, they were underperforming on standardized tests, graduation rates, and other key measures. But those numbers told only part of the story. It turned out that second graders performed on par with the national average but then something happened. By fourth grade, the students were falling behind by two grade levels, and by eighth grade, they were falling behind by four levels. The downward spiral just kept getting worse. Jessica and Jennifer determined that one reason might be that by the third grade, kids were becoming disengaged—and the answer might lie in technology.

Kids have technology all around them, and it's fun for them, but when they get to school, they're asked to put it away and stand in front of a chalkboard. They're bored by subjects such as math. So that was my daughters' entrepreneurial entry point: creating a computer game for third graders that would be fun and interactive and still drill them on the math basics. They called their entrepreneurial company Clairvoyant Technologies.

After getting some valuable help from their gaming whiz brother, Jessica and Jennifer submitted their idea to a local business plan competition and won some funding to develop a prototype. They were able to bring in a team of interns, build the prototype, and enlist two schools in Washington, D.C., to test it. One school was in the upscale Georgetown area, and the other was in a more disadvantaged area of southeast D.C. They liked the idea that they could test the effectiveness of their program in socioeconomically diverse classrooms.

But socioeconomics turned out *not* to be an issue. The issue in both schools was the inability of all the students to get online during class. So the greatest barrier was technological. They were five years or so ahead of their time. Without full online computer access in the classroom, the product could not succeed.

It was a disappointing result, but they took it as a valuable learning experience. They also found that although the product was effective and the need was great, they hadn't fully considered the market fit. In business, when you create a product, you scale it to the market realities, but this was difficult to do in the vast and somewhat chaotic educational system. Different schools had different stakeholders and different decision makers, usually based on politics.

I was proud of my daughters for deciding to take a chance and do something both creative and socially meaningful. And I'm especially proud that the experience didn't dissuade them from being entrepreneurs. They have the spirit.

I wanted them to develop that spirit, even as children. When they were young, I always encouraged them to have their own lemonade stands in different locations. I believed it would prepare them with the skills and courage to become good entrepreneurs.

One year Jessica, who was 12, wanted to attend the NASA Space Camp, and she needed $400. It was too late for a lemonade stand, so I suggested she raise money by putting together a presentation and giving it to five engineering organizations. She did a wonderful job, explaining to them that they could make a very small investment of $50 each to help train a future engineer. They responded and she raised $200. Her proud dad provided matching funds and she attended the camp.

I WRITE ABOUT MY daughters' experience because many people today wonder whether the opportunities that existed for my generation are available today. One of the most common sentiments I hear among young people is the concern that the opportunities have all been used up. They see immigrants of past generations "making it" in America but fear that the "Golden Door" of old is creaking shut for the young strivers. Actually, one of the main reasons I decided to write this book was to show young people that, in many ways, the environment for entrepreneurs and small business start-ups may be better than ever.

The good news is that there are many stories throughout the economy of individuals who without special resources had innovative ideas that through sheer will, hard work, and ingenuity they turned into American standards. These recent examples should inspire young people who wonder whether the American Dream is still available to them. In every case, these entrepreneurs started from scratch and staked out a niche in the American economy. *They identified a need and an opportunity and made it happen.*

Every immigrant who comes to America in search of a better life is asking himself or herself, "What can I do to make a difference in my new home?" There are many stories of immigrant prosperity—mine is one of them—but I am always struck by the fact that making huge amounts of money is not the driving motivation. Most people have a more basic ambition to create a good life for themselves and their families, to save enough to have a comfortable life, to send their kids to college. It is the middle-class dream, understanding that to be middle class in the United States seems like wealth in many other places around the world.

That being said, I'm here to tell you that the possibilities remain great, and that seems to be especially true for immigrants. We have to ask: why are immigrants so poised for business success? One key might be found in the words of Edward Roberts, who founded the MIT Entrepreneurship Center: "To immigrate is an entrepreneurial act."

Probably the most high-profile infusion of immigrant achievement has been in the technology arena. Earlier I mentioned Google's Sergey Brin. Another immigrant innovator is Yahoo's founder, Jerry Yang, who came from Taiwan with his mother and younger brother when he was 10, after his father died. At the time, he knew only one English word: "shoe." But Jerry's mother, a schoolteacher, pushed him to work hard and excel, and within three years, he was fluent in English. By the time he graduated from high school, he was first in his class.

The origin of the Yahoo concept came at Stanford, where Jerry was an engineering student. At first called "Jerry and David's Guide to the World Wide Web," they gave it the acronym Yahoo! for "Yet Another Hierarchical Officious Oracle." Yahoo! was an overnight sensation, and Yang became one of the wealthiest men in America. He didn't do it alone. "Living in Silicon Valley, we had access to mentors, entrepreneurs, venture capitalists, lawyers, and a very talented workforce," he told interviewer Tammy Hui. "Risk taking is a key ingredient to success and failure often a badge of honor. Growing up in this type of environment and hearing the stories of other entrepreneurial companies like Apple, HP, Intel, and Cisco gave me the courage to take an entrepreneurial path, innovate, and follow my passions."

In 2013, Yang resigned from Yahoo with plans to go out on his own as a start-up investor and mentor. He wants to keep innovating. Like a typical Chinese immigrant, Yang says his only regret is that he didn't study harder in school (though he studied pretty hard) and didn't pay more attention to his mother when he was young.

A particularly inspiring immigrant success story is that of Indra Nooyi, who came to the United States from India and is now CEO of PepsiCo. She tells the story of growing up in India, where her mother insisted that she and her siblings deliver a speech every night about what they wanted to be. The winner received a piece of chocolate. Nooyi credits her upbringing in

India for instilling in her the drive and moral strength to be successful—but she found the pinnacle of that success thanks to the United States. Many of the principles she has put to such great effect in her business life can be sourced to the values she learned in childhood as well as the new values of enterprise and adaptability she learned in America. Nooyi is proof that Americans embrace their new citizens when they make strong contributions to the community and the economy.

An immigrant entrepreneur named Foulis Peacock coined the phrase "immpreneur" to describe people who come to the United States, often with little money or resources, and build thriving businesses. Peacock created a website for budding immpreneurs to show them how to launch or grow existing businesses, how to use "foreignness" as an advantage, how to start a business, how to raise financing, how to sell and market products or services, and how to navigate the American business culture.

Peacock came to the United States from London 20 years ago after establishing a career in publishing. He became a contractor with *Forbes* magazine and then started a media representative company. In 2009, he started Immpreneur.com to support immigrant entrepreneurs.

Peacock has many stories to share of people who used their "foreign advantage" to recognize gaps in the market they could fill. A great example is Rohit Arora, a native of Delhi, India. Arora came to the United States in 2002 to get an MBA from Columbia University's School of Business. Shortly after graduating, he got a job with the management consulting firm Deloitte Consulting. While working on a project investigating the most profitable portfolios for banks, he made a surprising discovery: small businesses were the most profitable clients for banks when it came to loans and lines of credit, as well such products as checking accounts. When he dug deeper, he found that immigrant-founded start-ups were the fastest-growing category of small business in the country. He also discovered that few immigrant entrepreneurs sought bank loans and, on the whole, only a minority of banks had a policy of lending to such small businesses. Intrigued, he asked himself what was preventing small business owners and banks from working together. He found that many immigrant entrepreneurs avoided banks because they didn't understand how to navigate the system. (I could relate to that from my own early business experience.) Bankers considered the businesses too costly, cumbersome, and inefficient. What's more, they tended not to understand the cash-flow issues faced by many small, family-run immigrant businesses. So in 2007, Arora and his brother Ramit launched their business, calling it Biz2Credit, which enabled entrepreneurs to fill out all the documents and information that banks required and get access to them in one place. They also helped small businesses choose the best type of bank loan. "We became their virtual CFO," says Arora. In addition, business owners were able to get an answer quickly, rather than the usual lengthy wait at banks. Not long after launching the platform, the brothers added a management-support service, through which, for a monthly fee, entrepreneurs could receive online and phone help. Today, Biz2Credit is a $14-million business—a success story based on immigrants helping immigrants.

Ideas are everywhere, and sometimes they emanate from the most unlikely places. Hungarian Tom Szaky came to the United States as a freshman at Princeton University. While still a student, he came up with an original business idea: use worm castings—poop—to create a high-quality fertilizer and package it in recycled bottles. Eventually, that turned into a bigger concept, to turn all manner of unrecyclable waste products into new wares—everything from kites made from biscuit packets to backpacks created from juice pouches.

A decade later, Szaky heads a $13-million company with 75 employees and garbage collecting and recycling operations in eight countries. He says of becoming an entrepreneur in America: "The culture of America is built on the idea of encouraging entrepreneurship. Many other countries still have a fundamentally different attitude. If you're from a rich family, you stay rich. If you're poor, you stay poor. In places like Germany or France, the people have been there for hundreds and hundreds of years. That creates an entrenched society that restricts mobility. The culture here is about upward mobility and the importance of individual achievement. After all, the country is built on the efforts of immigrant entrepreneurs. What is the American Dream? That someone can come here with absolutely nothing and finish off as a multimillionaire. And that typically is facilitated through entrepreneurship."

Another inspiring story is that of Chobani Yogurt, which received the 2013 Ernst and Young World Entrepreneur Award. Hamdi Ulikays is an example of an immigrant who brought his knowledge and passion from back home and used it to great advantage in the United States. The son of Turkish sheep farmers, he came to America in 1997 to study at the University of Albany. On a visit from Turkey, Ulukaya's father complained that there were no good natural dairy products available. His father's comments lit a fire under Ulukaya. He realized that natural Greek yogurt was an untapped market in his new country. With the help of his brother, he spent two years creating and testing the perfect yogurt. In 2005, he took over a shuttered Kraft plant in central New York State and began production. It was an overnight success story—proof that if you find a niche and meet a need, the people will come. Only eight years later, Chobani is a $1-billion success story, with more than 3,000 employees around the world. Ulukaya credits American opportunity.

Not unlike my daughters, Shama Kabani, the 27-year-old founder and CEO of the Marketing Zen Group, was inspired by observing her parents. Kabani came with her family to the United States from India when she was nine years old. Her father drove a taxi, and her mother ran a Subway franchise. "I saw them work hard and doubly so because they were in a new country trying to adjust," Kabani says. She caught the bug early and started her own business when she was only 10, selling gift-wrapping paper. In 2008, she earned a master's in organizational communications from the University of Texas at Austin, where she wrote her thesis on the impact of Twitter and social media. She looked for a job in social media, her passion, but when she couldn't find one, she started her own company, the Marketing Zen Group, a full-service online marketing and digital PR firm. Through drive, work, and talent, Kabani built her firm into a $1-million enterprise. She celebrated her success the same year she became a naturalized citizen. "Pursue entrepreneurship if you have a passion for something," she says, a simple nugget of advice that has yielded great results for this young immigrant.

Often, the next generation stands up to take on the businesses their immigrant parents started. Julie Smolyansky, whose Russian immigrant father started Lifeway Foods in 1986, had to step in when she was just out of college after her father died suddenly of a heart attack. When Michael Smolyansky immigrated to Chicago from the Soviet Union, he had $100 to his name, but he saw a need. Although the Russian immigrant community was growing, no businesses were catering to them. He decided to start a deli to give them a taste of home. Working as an engineer by day, he saved for two years before he had enough money to open a small store. His wife, Ludmilla, began working at the business during the day while Michael kept his engineering job and took over at night. The business grew, and they began visiting food shows overseas to get new ideas. During one trip, they found a drink they had loved as children—a yogurt-like concoction called kefir, which was impossible to find at home. They decided on the spot to begin producing the drink in their basement. That was the origin of Lifeway Foods. When they began selling the drink on the open market, they gained a lot of publicity and some big clients, including Whole Foods, followed by Wegmans and Kroger.

Michael Smolyansky would be proud to know that his daughter has grown the company to an $80-million business. She believes that the key to success is the bedrock set of values that comes naturally to immigrants—including being conservative. Her parents were very frugal, and they lived simply, even as the business grew. As Julie sees it, their success came because they found a way to reach out to their own community. "Many immigrants can probably find a similar situation to my father's," she advises. "Search for a staple from your country that's popular, and bring it to America. There's an instant ethnic market here. If you do it properly, you can create interest outside of that ethnic group."

If you look out across the American landscape, you'll find countless "maker" stories just like these. Success isn't necessarily measured by being multimillion-dollar companies, either. There is a treasure trove of little businesses, as small as a farmer's market stand, a laundromat, a beauty parlor, or a food truck, that have benefited from the American Dream.

Many organizations have risen up to foster this amazing trend. For example, AnewAmerica Community Corporation in Berkeley, California, which serves aspiring immigrant entrepreneurs throughout California, has created an intensive "virtual incubator," a three-year program for immigrant entrepreneurs. AnewAmerica's model integrates business incubation, asset building, and social responsibility. Entrepreneurs and their families receive a package of comprehensive services for three years to meet their cultural and linguistic needs. AnewAmerica is part of the vibrant emerging microenterprise trend I spoke of earlier.

WHEN I LOOK AROUND, I ask, what do the world's greatest entrepreneurs have in common? One thing I've noticed is the same level of passion and engagement that I've seen in Jessica and Jennifer.

Entrepreneurs are people who have exceptional confidence and strong self-esteem. They may not have been the best and brightest students—I certainly wasn't—but, somewhere in their developmental years, they internalized a message that they could do anything they set out to do. They believe in themselves.

Entrepreneurs are visionary. They go forward even if all the dots aren't yet connected—trusting that they'll connect later. Steve Jobs, the great entrepreneur and founder of Apple, who died in 2012, gave a memorable commencement speech in 2005 at Stanford University where he talked about connecting the dots. Recalling his own life, where he'd made some unconventional choices, including dropping out of school at one point, he told the graduates, "You can't connect the dots looking forward; you can only connect them looking backward. So you have to trust that the dots will somehow connect in your future. You have to trust in something: your gut, destiny, life, karma, whatever. This approach has never let me down, and it has made all the difference in my life."

Entrepreneurs have courage. As Jennifer put it when I asked her, "Being an entrepreneur takes gumption. You have to walk into unfamiliar situations and put everything on the line. You have to have mental fortitude and say to yourself, 'All they can do is say no—why don't I ask?'"

Entrepreneurs have heart. We often hear about the most successful entrepreneurs—people such as Bill Gates and Sergey Brin—who have become phenomenally wealthy. But most entrepreneurs are not among the superrich, and their motivation seems to be more about love than money. If you go into something with the primary goal to make a lot of money, you won't necessarily succeed. But if you create from the heart, success often follows.

In the United States, 21 percent of high-net-worth individuals made their money through entrepreneurship, and many other nations are following suit. But money alone was rarely the motivation.

Writing in *Psychology Today*, Adrian Furnham posed the question of why migrants seem to have an entrepreneurial flair. He suggests that one answer may be the types of people who migrate. He said that studies of those who choose to migrate show that they "tend to be different from those who don't. They have a different pattern of motivation, abilities and adjustment. They are hungrier, more risk taking, more hardy. Migration is difficult. There are many hurdles to cross including language, money and the law. You have to be very determined just to get there. The experience of hardship, rejection and setback toughens you up. These are life events that all entrepreneurs have to get used to."

Fuhrham also points to external factors, such as the strength of social networks in immigrant communities. But the key factors seem to be internal: personality, values, and motivation. He observes that "often, successful native entrepreneurs were themselves outsiders in some way. If you come from a minority religious group; have a family very different from all around you; if you look different, or are disabled in some regard, you can feel a stranger in your own country. This can be similar to the spur that so many migrants feel . . . and is part of the story of nearly every entrepreneur."

Nassim Taleb, a Lebanese American author and scholar, speculated on the success of Lebanese-born immigrants with this thought: "The idea is that in a natural setting, anything natural, anything organic, anything biological, up to a point, reacts a lot better *to* stressors than without . . . A little bit of adversity results in a little bit more performance in anything." It is a simple notion but perfectly credible. Immigrants struggle; they have unique stresses. And those stresses can make them stronger.

Study after study finds that immigrants have embraced the entrepreneurial path. Every time this happens, America wins. According to the Global Entrepreneurship Monitor, first-generation immigrants to the United States are 27 percent more likely to start businesses than nonimmigrants. Some 63 percent of these immigrants were in the top one-third of U.S. earners, compared to 50 percent of nonimmigrant entrepreneurs. One interesting factor that the report notes is that immigrants are more prone to spotting opportunities and less afraid of failure. Based on my own experience, I suspect this is in large part due to the special mind-set of an immigrant. You come to a new country seeking a better future for yourself and your family and have to leap through many hoops to get there—including language, cultural differences, and difficulties integrating into communities. These challenges strengthen you and make you more open to taking risks. You say, "What do I have to lose? I might as well go for it!"

The 2013 Gallup World Poll confirms some of these assumptions about immigrants, especially if they live in prosperous economies such as the United States. Gallup finds that immigrants are more likely than native-born residents to have three characteristics that also happen to differentiate entrepreneurs from the rest: they feel optimistic even when things go wrong, they never give up, and they are willing to take risks.

Karen Gordon Mills, who was the Small Business Administration administrator during the early years of the Obama administration, writes that the entrepreneurial spirit of America's small business owners is heightened by the influence of immigrants. "Immigrants over-index in entrepreneurship," she notes. "According to a study by the Partnership for a New American Economy, immigrants are more than twice as likely to start a business in the United States as non-immigrants, and in 2011, immigrants started 28 percent of all new businesses while only accounting for 13 percent of the U.S. population. These businesses inject vitality and a global vision into our economy. Immigrant-owned businesses are exporting and opening up markets around the globe. New immigrants ensure diversity and new ideas in our society. Approximately 26 percent of all U.S.-based Nobel laureates over the past 50 years were foreign-born. And immigrants are strengthening our communities, fueling job creation and fostering innovation in key industries. According to the Partnership for a New American Economy study, every additional 100 foreign-born worker in STEM fields with advanced degrees from U.S. universities are associated with an additional 262 jobs among American workers."

I've painted a picture of opportunity here, but we also have to face facts. It's not always possible for budding entrepreneurs who want to live in America to come here. That reality was the basis for an astonishingly creative enterprise for two men. Dario Mutabdzija, an immigrant from Sarajevo, and Max Marty, the son of Cuban immigrants, set out to find a way that aspiring immigrants could connect with American enterprise while they were still trying to get papers. Their start-up, called Blueseed, involves a large ocean vessel to be situated 12 miles offshore in international waters near Silicon Valley. Entrepreneurs from all over the world will live and work on the ship, which is scheduled for launch in 2014. With high-speed Internet on board and ferry trips to Silicon Valley, these entrepreneurs hope to do business with Silicon Valley and take full advantage of American opportunity. So far, more than 1,500 entrepreneurs from 500 start-ups in 70 countries have applied.

OVER THE YEARS, I've broadened my definition of what it means to be an entrepreneur. Technically speaking, I long ago moved from being an entrepreneur to building medium-sized businesses. But I've realized that the entrepreneurial spirit is what matters. You can be the largest company in the country and still be entrepreneurial. Entrepreneurship is everywhere. I subscribe to the idea put forth by the Consortium for Entrepreneurial Education that lifelong learning and openness to new ideas and opportunities keep us all in a mind-set to grow and thrive. I've been in business more than 30 years, but I still keep that entrepreneurial spark lit. I think of every new business direction in my companies as if it was a mini start-up.

My daughter Jessica describes the entrepreneurial spirit this way: "You get to choose your own adventure." Both Jessica and Jennifer have the entrepreneurial spirit, and it's going strong. It has survived many ups and downs, and it lives in their hearts. For example, Jennifer has set aside the start-up process for the time being to join a company as a product manager. But look at the company she chose—a thriving entrepreneurial start-up called GetWellNetwork, which develops innovative technologies to make the experience of hospital patients better, more personal, and more educational. The entrepreneurial spirit is a basic job requirement there.

Jessica, with two colleagues, has just launched a technology start-up called Luminate Health, which provides an easy way for patients to access, manage, and understand their laboratory results. With venture capital support, Luminate Health is working with its first lab customers.

It's not accidental that my daughters directed their entrepreneurship first to education and now to health care. Those choices say a lot about their values. Jessica has told me that Maggie and I instilled in them as children the ability to value the right thing. "We were always reminded about the importance of caring for one another and giving what you can to others," she said. "We were taught that by reaching out, we could change other people's lives."

One other thing: their upbringing taught them to dream. When they were young, there wasn't much money, so they had to use their imagination. Instead of playing with the latest expensive toy, they created worlds that transported them into endlessly entertaining adventures. The entrepreneurial spirit was born in their imaginations, and they know that as long as they can imagine something, it becomes possible.

Marriage of my mother and father in Nanjing, China (1936).

Me as a two-year-old in the park with my mother.

Me as a high school student.

As a second lieutenant platoon leader in Jinmen, an island five miles from mainland China, I was in charge of 40 LVTs, a class of amphibious war vehicle (1974).

Maggie and I were instantly drawn to each other.

Marrying Maggie was the best day of my life (1976).

David and Mary Miller and their children taught Maggie and me about the American way of reaching out to newcomers. They were our second family.

When I graduated with a masters of science, I gave my hat and tassel to Maggie. I couldn't have done it without her (1978).

In 1991, I received the National Small Business Prime Contractor of the Year Award, presented at the White House by President George H.W. Bush.

In 2001, I had the thrilling experience of being given a ride in an F-15 fighter jet. MTI produced hardware for the F-15 program.

In 2007, I was appointed by President George W. Bush as associate administrator of the Office of Government Contracting and Business Development.

Our family prospered in America. At my son, John's, wedding in 2013, we celebrated with four generations, including my mother, my daughters, Jessica and Jennifer, and their husbands, and my new grandson, Max.

eight

EMBRACING THE GIFT OF DIVERSITY

Many people who have visited Eglin Air Force Base over the years have passed by Jo's Tailor Shop near the east gate. Jo, a Filipino immigrant, started her shop in 1966 and is still running it as she enters her ninetieth year. Hers is one of those quiet American immigrant stories that tugs at the heart and demonstrates an iron will and a strong work ethic. Jo's backstory, as well as the story of how she ended up working for Elgin Air Force Base, is quite moving. Her story, recounted by Scott T. Jackson for the *Business Magazine of NW Florida*, is one of remarkable bravery. During World War II, Jo's family members risked their lives helping American prisoners of war who had survived the Bataan death march. Jo's father, Teodoro, operated a restaurant near the POW camp, and he enlisted his family to help the prisoners, telling them that if they were caught, they would be tortured and killed. All Filipinos knew the terrible risks. They had seen collaborators waterboarded and brutally murdered, had watched them being made to dig their own graves before being shot. Nevertheless, with their father's encouragement,

Jo, who was 18, and her six-year-old brother Teddy established a routine. They would approach the camp, and Jo, who was quite pretty, would flirt with the guards and distract them while Teddy crawled under the barbed wire and delivered bags of food, clothing, and medicine for malaria and beriberi. They undoubtedly saved many lives through their bravery.

After the war, Jo married one of the POWs she had helped, moved to the United States, and became a citizen. When her husband was assigned to Eglin Air Force Base, they settled in Niceville (a town a few miles from Fort Walton Beach). Jo worked at Eglin's tailor shop for several years, making uniforms, before starting her own business in 1966. Word of mouth helped her business thrive, and her service to the POWs has never been forgotten. In 1984, when her brother Teddy was having trouble getting permanent residence status in the United States, a group of former POWs intervened, petitioning President Reagan to make a special allowance for the man who as a young boy had once helped keep them alive.

Jo's story is an inspiration to all of us in the area. She is one of the "makers" who helps create our rich business tapestry. Her life experience also underscores the wonderful diversity of our nation—the fact that people from every corner of the earth can be part of the same American Dream. I love telling stories like Jo's because they are such uplifting examples of the way diversity is woven into the character of America. Another of my favorite examples is story of the family of Jeb Bush.

I've always been a big admirer of Bush, who was governor of Florida between 1999 and 2007. I met him a few times when he traveled across the state, and in 2006, he appointed me to serve on the Committee for a Sustainable Emerald Coast. His commonsense approach to economic growth is very appealing, and he has a very warm, personable manner.

Bush is trustworthy on issues related to immigration and cultural diversity, because he lives them every day. As the husband of an immigrant,

I think he probably knows a lot more than most native-born Americans about our diverse identity.

Bush's story is very compelling. In 1970, as a high school senior, he participated in a student exchange program in the town of Leon, Mexico. There he met Columba Garnica de Gallo, also a senior. Although Bush was barely out of boyhood, he declared it love at first sight. A year later, Columba moved to Southern California for college, and Bush went to the University of Texas, where he majored in Latin American studies. After a four-year long-distance relationship, they were married in 1974.

Recalling his personal journey in his book, *Immigration Wars: Forging an American Solution*, which he coauthored with Clint Bolick, Bush wrote, "Thanks to my wife, I became bicultural and bilingual, and my life is better because of it. For the first time in my life, I learned what the immigrant experience was, and I grew to appreciate her desire to learn English and embrace American values, while still retaining her love for the traditions of Mexico."

Columba Bush became an American citizen in 1979, and for Bush the naturalization ceremony was deeply meaningful. "It is a fundamentally American experience," he wrote, "to see people of every nationality, every background, all coming together to swear their loyalty to our great country. Most have tears in their eyes, and all of them aspire to a better life than what they left behind."

The Bushes have instilled all-American values in their children, especially the obligation and privilege of public service. Their son, George Prescott Bush, is currently carrying on the family tradition, running for Texas land commissioner and highlighting his status as a young, Hispanic, Spanish-speaking candidate.

In large part because of his personal experience, Bush has become an outspoken advocate for opening more opportunities for immigrants, as well as changing negative stereotypes that still exist. These anti-immigration attitudes gained some momentum after September 11 when fear and suspicion of foreignness were high. The cause was bolstered by a sense even among immigration supporters that we had to do something to rein in the ever-growing number of undocumented residents. Bush promotes an opportunity-based, not a fear-based, mind-set.

There is no question that Bush believes that immigrants provide great value to the nation. He is committed to helping Americans see that value, too, and he proposes that one way of doing that is to encourage a demand-driven system—that is, enabling more highly skilled workers and aspiring entrepreneurs to come to America.

Backed by clear evidence of the contribution immigrants have made to the American economy and culture, many people are focusing on the need to attract more highly skilled workers. Software entrepreneur Jim Manzi writes in *National Affairs* that we would be wise to approach immigration as a way of recruiting new talent and "set up recruiting offices looking for the best possible talent everywhere: from Mexico City to Beijing to Helsinki to Calcutta. Australia and Canada have demonstrated the practicality of skills-based immigration policies for many years. We should improve upon their example by using testing and other methods to apply a basic tenet of all human capital–intensive organizations managing for the long term: Always pick talent over skill. It would be great for America as a whole to have, say, 500,000 smart, motivated people move here each year with the intention of becoming citizens."

Among those who want to encourage more highly skilled workers is Edward Roberts, the David Sarnoff professor of management of technology at MIT Sloan and founder and chair of the Martin Trust Center. According to Roberts, "Data on fifty years of MIT entrepreneurs, and many studies of engineering manpower, demonstrate that a very high fraction of our new technical manpower, and a higher fraction of our high-tech entrepreneurs, are foreign-born. Providing an easy path for their permanent stay in the United States provides the most significant boost to our jobs and economic growth of any economic policy. Foreign graduate students who are enrolled in our entrepreneurship programs . . . tell me that they have problems with their visas from the outset, providing a negative message from the United States about their desirability. Unless they get a sponsor, they have big problems in remaining beyond their student visas. They encounter major issues if they want to start a company on their own here, needing to learn rules, laws and gambits around our regulations." Roberts believes that there are many ways to help alleviate these barriers if only we have the will to do so.

A research report by the Missouri-based Kauffman Foundation outlined practical recommendations that would enable talented international students to launch job-creating ventures in the United States. These include allowing students in undergraduate or graduate programs to actively participate as employees or owners in a "Qualifying Startup Student Venture," expanding eligibility for the 17-month optional practical training extension, currently granted only to STEM students, to include students actively involved as employees or owners of businesses as part of entrepreneurship studies and streamlining the H-1B visa process for principals of start-up businesses. By reducing the burden for emerging entrepreneurs, the nation gains valuable new talent.

As Shayan Zadeh, an immigrant from Iran who is the founder and CEO of Zoosk, an online dating service, wrote in the *Wall Street Journal*, "As an American by choice, I am proud of our country's history of welcoming the tired, the poor and the 'huddled masses' who were starving or persecuted and came here create a better life. But I'm baffled by the fact that we are turning away the skilled masses that are hungry only for work, even as our economy remains stagnant."

These ideas support the strong case made by Thomas Friedman, who writes, "I think keeping a constant flow of legal immigrants into our country—whether they wear blue collars or lab coats—is the key to keeping us ahead of China. Because when you mix all of these energetic, high-aspiring people with a democratic system and free markets, magic happens. If we hope to keep that magic, we need immigration reform that guarantees that we will always attract and retain, in an orderly fashion, the world's first-round aspirational and intellectual draft choices."

The good news is that a large majority of Americans favor encouraging diversity in our communities and workplaces. A survey by the Rockefeller Foundation, titled "Building an All-In Nation: A View from the American Public," found that 69 percent of those surveyed agreed that "a bigger, more diverse workforce will lead to more economic growth" and that "diverse workplaces and schools will help make American businesses more innovative and competitive."

The point is that America is, by its nature, diverse and was founded with immigrants in mind. As Michael Barone, author of *Shaping Our Nation: How Surges of Migration Transformed America and Its Politics*, writes, the Founding Fathers built the idea of diversity into the Constitution. "The Framers of the Constitution and the Bill of Rights were well aware of the different religious and cultural backgrounds of the different states," he writes. "They were determined to create a strong federal government but one whose powers would be limited in order to reduce cultural conflict and preserve zones of autonomy. This was a revolutionary approach to constitution-making, adopted when England still required public officials to be members of the established Church of England and when, in all European nations, Jews were subject to civil disabilities, including prohibition on holding public office." Barone notes that the framers' formula of limited government and individual rights "has provided a ready and useful template for the accommodation of diverse peoples."

In the summer of 2013, a coalition of 420 companies, including business and industry associations and state and local chambers of commerce, sent a letter to Congress, addressed to Speaker John Boehner and Minority Leader Nancy Pelosi, urging them to pass immigration reform as an imperative to a more vibrant business environment. They wrote:

> Thought leaders from across the ideological spectrum agree that enacting immigration reform now will accelerate U.S. economic growth at a critical time when it has struggled to recover, and will help to enable sustained growth for decades to come. Done right, reform will also serve to protect and complement our U.S. workforce, generating greater productivity and economic activity that will lead to new innovations, products, businesses, and jobs in communities across the U.S.
>
> We are united in the belief that we can and must do better for our economy and country by modernizing our immigration system . . . Failure to act is not an option. We can't afford to be content and watch a generation-old immigration system work more and more against our overall national interest. Instead, we urge Congress to remain mindful of the clear benefits to our economy if we succeed, and work together and with us to achieve real, pro-growth immigration reform.

Even the League of Women Voters has gotten into the act, publishing research that highlights the advantages of a diverse population, including the facts that more diverse companies have more business success, whether large or small; more diverse juries take more issues into consideration as a group; and individuals participating in more diverse groups take more issues into consideration as individuals, regardless of group considerations.

From the founding of our nation, there have always been negative undercurrents about immigrants. In our time, stereotypes exist, suggesting that immigrants are part of the welfare state, that they are taking jobs from native-born Americans, and that they keep to their own communities and don't care about becoming "real" Americans. I hope I've helped to dispel some of those notions with this book. There is a growing body of research data showing just the opposite.

The New Immigrant Survey is a study conducted over a period of years, cooperatively produced by government agencies, universities, and business leaders. It is a multicohort prospective-retrospective panel study of new legal immigrants to the United States, a multiyear study by a group of government agencies, independent research organizations, and universities. It shows that, on average, immigrants—especially those from strong families—perform as well as or better than native-born Americans in measures of education, productivity, employment, and home ownership.

Another important study comes by way of the George W. Bush Institute. Like his brother, our former president has always been outspoken about the role of immigrants in creating an opportunity society. "America has never been united by blood or birth or soil," he said, addressing the point. "We are bound by ideals that move us beyond our backgrounds, lift us above our interests, and teach us what it means to be citizens. Every child must be taught these principles. Every citizen must uphold them, and every immigrant, by embracing these ideals, makes our country more, not less, American." The institute, founded by the president and Mrs. Bush in 2009, has made a serious study of immigrant trends, especially the underlying reasons that many immigrants thrive in America.

The first reason is social. Far from the stereotype that immigrants are a drain on the social order, the Bush Institute found that in 2011, 58.3 percent of immigrants were married, compared to 46.5 percent of native-born Americans. Furthermore, 62.3 percent of immigrant households were headed by a married couple in 2011, compared to 57.9 percent of native households.

The marriage data are an important measure of success, as economic studies have found strong evidence that married couples, on average, are more productive and enjoy higher standards of living, higher incomes, and better health outcomes, compared to single individuals.

The second reason cited by the institute is immigrants' role in the labor force. Immigrants have consistently had a more prominent role in the labor force than is commonly appreciated, given their representation in the country's population. The trend is interesting: in 2003, 11.7 percent of all U.S. residents were immigrants, but immigrants represented 14.3 percent of the labor force. Throughout the 2000s, both these proportions grew, and by 2011, immigrants accounted for approximately 13 percent of the country's population and 15.9 percent of the civilian labor force. In 2011, approximately 67.1 percent of immigrants 16 years of age and older were in the labor force, compared to only 62.9 percent of native-born citizens. The institute concludes that "by and large immigrants want to work. This allows them to earn a living and helps our economy grow. The growth in the U.S. labor force over the past decade would have been much smaller if not for immigrants. More than half of the growth in new workers over the past decade is attributable to immigrants."

According to the institute, "One widely unknown benefit of immigration is the positive effect immigrants have on the educational attainment of natives." The institute cites research by Jennifer Hunt showing that when more immigrants are present in the population, natives are more likely to complete high school. Hunt's research finds that "an increase of one percentage point in the share of immigrants in the population aged 11–64 increases the probability that natives aged 11–17 eventually complete 12 years of schooling by 0.3 percentage points"—not an insignificant number.

These statistics are not surprising in light of what we've already described as a strong work ethic, entrepreneurial spirit, and ambition among immigrants. They underscore the point that we have much to be thankful for in our diverse society, and much of that diversity is the positive infusion of new talent and patriotism from other lands.

THERE ARE EXISTENTIAL questions at the heart of America that get asked again and again. Those questions are as follows: Is our country a place where people from a multitude of nations, cultures, and ethnicities come together and meld their individuality into a common national identity? Or is it a patchwork of cultures and ethnicities that live many different ways and speak many different languages but share a common Constitution?

I believe that the answer lies somewhere in the middle. First of all, the United States is much more than a political system or a set of constitutional precepts. Americans have a very strong social identity, of which our diversity is a part. When I came here as an immigrant, at first my identity was very much Chinese. I didn't have language skills or a community, and I still had much to learn about America. In a sense, I think settling in places where there were few immigrants from Asia helped me assimilate faster. In addition, I developed a very strong desire to become an American, and so did Maggie. We saw the United States as a place we could call home. We cherished our cultural heritage but didn't see it as separate. We viewed it as a contribution we were making to the diverse American tapestry.

It has not always been apparent that immigration surges would turn out well for America. For example, in my own state of Florida, there was great anxiety when Cuban refugees began to flock there in the 1960s. Officials loudly predicted a decline in the economy and quality of life, especially in cities such as Miami. Instead, the opposite happened. The Cuban infusion was responsible for turning Dade County into the fastest-growing economy in the nation. When Americans embrace the diverse contributions of immigrants, everyone prospers.

Because I am a businessman, much of my focus has been on immigrant business success stories. But we can't deny the tremendous impact that immigrants have made on every corner of American society. It is impossible to imagine American politics, literature, science, entertainment, and sports without them. Consider how immigrant voices have shaped American politics. Congresswoman Ileana Ros-Lehtinen, a Cuban immigrant in my home state of Florida, has served since 1982 as the first Hispanic woman in Congress. Madeleine Albright, whose distinguished career includes being the secretary of state, began her life in Czechoslovakia. Arnold Schwarzenegger, the Austrian-born movie star who served as governor of California, is a true American success story. Many people have said that if it were not for the edict against foreign-born citizens being president, he would make a fine candidate for the highest office in the land.

Of the 87 current astronauts, seven hail from other countries, including Costa Rica, India, England, Spain, Peru, and Australia. Their dreams of exploring other worlds began with their own travels to this country.

Immigrant contributions to American literature have been especially meaningful, giving voice and heart to the human struggle. Modern literature is full of their wonderful work—Khaled Hosseini, from Afghanistan, who gave us *The Kite Runner*; Jhumpa Lahiri, from India, who gave us *Namesake*; Ha Jin, from China, who gave us *Waiting*; and Azar Nafisi, from

Iran, who gave us *Reading Lolita in Tehran*—among others. Through them, we have gained priceless understanding of the multiplicity of cultures.

It's hard to imagine American sports without an immigrant infusion. Baseball, the "American pastime," is filled with immigrants. In fact, according to Major League Baseball, 28 percent of all current rosters are composed of players born in other countries. That includes Dominican Republic–born David Ortiz, who led the Boston Red Sox to victory in 2013. He was aided by closing pitcher Koji Uehara from Japan.

Even our current Miss America, Nina Davuluri, is the daughter of immigrants. Miss America is considered a role model for young girls, and Davuluri has embraced that role as a spokeswoman for diversity and opportunity. "That's just something that we grew up with," she says. "Regardless of your gender, your race, your ethnicity, socioeconomic status, anyone can truly follow their dreams, become anything they want—not only Miss America. That is the whole ideal of the American Dream, and that is what I am living right now."

Davuliri is part of a promising trend that I have seen repeatedly, including in my own family, that is, the wonderful character of the next generation. Overall, children of immigrants have higher incomes, more education, and more home ownership than average. Like my children, they consider themselves "typical" Americans but with an added benefit.

Karen Kaminsky of the New York Immigration Coalition expressed a sentiment I have heard from my own daughters: "There is a continued faith that life here can present opportunities if you work hard for them. I think you have to have that faith in order to uproot yourself. I think if you do that as parents, your children are going to sense that."

I like the term "American by choice," which is the way immigrants often describe themselves. That choice is fully made, with great commitment and joy. It's not easy to become a U.S. citizen. It requires hard work and study, including a test that might challenge most Americans. In one study conducted by the Center for the Study of the American Dream at Xavier University in Cincinnati, only 65 percent of native-born Americans could get the required six out of 10 right answers when asked similar questions in a telephone poll. These are questions that go to the heart of what makes us American—such as how a bill becomes law, the meaning of due process, identifying the three branches of government, and naming the significant events that shaped our nation.

Maybe there is a natural tendency toward complacency when you don't have to strive to become American. But it isn't just a matter of answering questions on a test. The experience of becoming a citizen makes an everlasting impression on a person—like a stamp on the heart. You never forget it. Citizenship remains precious for the rest of your life.

nine

BELIEVING IN AMERICA . . . WHO ARE THE GUARDIANS?

The year I came to America was a time of great upheaval. The president of the United States had just been forced to resign under threat of impeachment. The nation was still struggling to end a long, devastating war in Southeast Asia. The economy was steeped in a recession. The energy crisis was on the near horizon, and in the next year, unemployment would reach 8.5 percent. Congress had a 30 percent approval rating. American youth felt disenfranchised. Commentators were saying that America was in decline. Still I came. I wasn't naive about America. I could see the problems. But somehow I trusted that the United States would rise above them. I understood that this young country was a work in progress.

My faith in America turned out to be warranted. The 1980s, opening with Ronald Reagan's vision of "morning in America," heralded a new era of prosperity and optimism. In the next 20 years, the Cold War ended, the economy prospered (especially in the Sun Belt, where I lived), the personal computer and digital technology changed the world, and a new openness toward immigration infused the country with some of the best and bright-est innovators of our times. The shift from a sense of decline to a sense of optimism was palpable—and it demonstrated for me a central truth about America: it loves a comeback.

I began this book with a question: Is the American Dream alive or dead? The question came from the feelings of pessimism that enveloped our nation in the wake of the financial crisis of 2008. It came from polls of young people who worried that they'd never have a chance to realize the American Dream. They wondered whether working hard could lead to a good life, perhaps even a life better than that of their parents. I wanted to send a message to our youth to tell them that the great gift of opportunity that I received as a young man was still available to them today—and, to take it a step further, that the future might be better than ever.

This isn't an empty promise. I believe it, and the evidence is clear in every chapter of this book. But especially here in this last chapter, I want to offer a vision of America based on the greatness I know is in the heart of our nation.

One factor is immigration. I have described immigrants as being the guardians of the American Dream. That is not to say that native-born Americans don't play this role as well. But in my own life and the lives of others, I have seen undeniable evidence that the immigrant mind-set and character embody the American Dream, making us uniquely equipped as guardians:

- We choose America freely and gladly.

- We study the American way with reverence for our adopted system.

- We are resilient—stubborn even. The gifts of democracy may not have been our birthright, but we achieved them through our strong desire and effort.

- We know that hard work is the partner of hope, and it is important what we can do for our country—not the other way around.

Modern immigrants understand more than ever that America is not a big, warm blanket of security. It is an engine that propels us to invent and create. Many people have the wrong idea of the immigrant promise because of the poem by Emma Lazarus that was placed on a plaque on the Statue of Liberty. Its words are famous; every school child learns them: "Give me your tired, your poor, your huddled masses yearning to breathe free, the wretched refuse of your teeming shore. Send these, the homeless, tempest-tossed to me." But that poem was not written until long after the Statue of Liberty was erected in the New York Harbor, and it is only a tiny piece of the story. We could just as well say, "Bring me your dreamers and innovators, the seekers and strivers longing for an opportunity and energized by your soaring possibilities."

When I made the choice to come to America, I was not fleeing an impossible situation. I was not destitute. I was not alone and without family.

I was not suffering. My life and liberty were not at risk. I was not homeless or tempest-tossed. I made the choice because I was looking for something *more*, and America represented that hope.

Many people do not fully appreciate that those of us growing up outside the United States are always conscious of America. Its bright promise and can-do attitude pervade the world. As a young man in Taiwan, I saw the people of my nation become captivated by, of all things, baseball. There is nothing more American than baseball, and maybe that's why it has become so popular in Asian countries. For us, that happened with a Little League team that became national heroes. For several years, the Gold Dragons of Taiwan were unbeatable internationally, even in America. The Taiwanese were delirious with joy. Not only did we pour our national pride into the fates of these young boys but also we reveled in wearing the mantle of America's defining sport. No young Taiwanese baseball player, if he were honest, could resist the dream of some day playing for the New York Yankees. The success of the Gold Dragons thrilled us. It was as if we could vicariously and in this small way take on some of America's magic.

America is the only country in the world that is so generous with its dream, which is why most immigrants want to assimilate its values and why their children, like my own, are so glad to call themselves "typical Americans."

One of the most appealing and also most promising characteristics of America is that it is an experiment. By its nature, an experiment is open-ended and future oriented. If one element fails, there are still many other opportunities for success. I willingly acknowledge that America has problems, some of them great. But they never outweigh the astonishing possibility that is embedded in this unique experiment. In *America the Beautiful: Rediscovering What Made This Nation Great*, Ben Carson, MD, captures this promise beautifully, writing, "In its relatively short history, America has transformed humankind's existence on earth. Among the many factors involved in our success was the conscious creation of an atmosphere conducive to innovation and hard work . . . for the first time in the world, a nation was envisioned that was 'of, by, and for the people.'"

This bedrock principle bestows ownership of the dream on each and every one of us. We can never look at our government or economy and despair, because it is up to us to make things better. As long as we have ideas, innovation, and the will to succeed, we can continue to shape America. That is why if a young person tells me he or she is disillusioned about our country's future, I can say, "Well, then, change it." It is the same thing I said to myself when I was a young man with no money struggling to start a company. I knew the future was in my own hands.

So, today, as I contemplate our coming years and the strength of our dreams, I want to share the reasons why my belief in America is stronger than ever.

1. America's openness protects and inspires us.

When Maggie and I made our cross-country drive across the United States in the 1970s, we were strangers in a strange land—marveling at the wide-open plains and the friendliness we encountered. People accepted us and helped us despite our poor English. The idea of taking such a road trip is uniquely American. So is the ability to easily relocate from one part of the country to another. If we had stayed in Taiwan, it's unlikely that we would ever have left Taipei. But in America we were free to pull up stakes and move from Missouri to Florida without any bureaucratic complications. Our children never felt a necessity to stay in Florida once they reached adulthood. Our two daughters live in Washington, D.C., and our son lives in San Francisco. We all travel regularly to see each other. We are protected and inspired by our common identity.

In America, we are proud of our home states, but most of us can envision belonging in any of the 50 states. We have full confidence that if we move—say, to Silicon Valley or Chicago or Seattle—we'll find that government and business play by the same rules. We won't feel like strangers.

I contrast this strong sense of identity with the European Union. The EU was established to bring European countries under one umbrella. The motto was "unity in diversity," which sounds almost American. But when you dig deeper, you find that an actual European identity is hard to find beyond the common currency. As the noted international scholar and commentator Francis Fukiyama put it, there is "a failure in European identity. That is to say, there was never a successful attempt to create a European sense of identity, and a European sense of citizenship that would define the obligations, responsibilities, duties and rights that Europeans have to one another beyond simply the wording of the different treaties that were signed. The EU in many respects was created as a technocratic exercise for the purposes of economic efficiency. What we can see now is that economic and post-national values are not enough to really buy into this community together."

A sense of identity—as we state it, "one nation under God"—is organic. It's built into our national DNA. While we may identify ourselves by our states ("I am a Texan") or by our family origins ("My family is Italian"), our national identity is more fundamental. Traveling anywhere in the world we say, "I am an American." One is less likely to hear "I am a European" and more likely to hear Europeans identify themselves as French, English, Italian, or German.

America was built on this identity. It was not superimposed. That's not to say that the EU might not eventually reach that state of common identity. But thousands of years of nationalism are not easily overcome.

2. In America, the welcome mat is open to all, regardless of who you are.

Colin Powell, the son of immigrant parents from Jamaica, distinguished himself many times over as an American hero. I was touched by a story he told about what he called the "welcoming nature" of the American people. He was speaking to a group of Brazilian exchange students, and he asked them to tell him about their experiences. One of the students related an incident that occurred when 12 of the exchange students went to a restaurant in Chicago. After finishing their meal, they realized they didn't have enough money to cover the bill. This scared them. They didn't know what would happen. They finally got up enough nerve to tell their waitress, and she went away to speak with her boss. When she came back, she told them that the manager had said it was OK. They were stunned by this but still worried that the difference would come out of the waitress's pocket. She smiled and said, "No, the manager said he is glad you are here in the United States.

He hopes you are having a good time, and he hopes you are learning all about us. He said it's on him." In telling the story, Powell added, "That's the America I believe in; that's the America the world wants to believe in." I agree. It reminds me of being a poor and lonely young student in Missouri and being embraced by David and Mary. Their wonderful support probably changed my life. I assure you that most immigrants have stories to tell of that stereotypical smiling American who reached out to them when they were feeling adrift and insecure.

America's welcoming nature is not reflected only in these anecdotal stories, nor is it reserved just for newcomers or visitors. Our country was founded on the idea that everyone deserves a fair shot. This "everyone" might be a child born in Arkansas or Bangladesh or Taiwan. Each citizen is welcome to rise as high as his or her dreams. Our Constitution protects every citizen regardless of race or class or origins and calls this equality "self-evident."

By contrast, many nations in the world remain homogenous and uneasy with outsiders. Consider Japan, which is a modern and in many ways very innovative nation. Yet only 1.7 percent of the population is foreign born.

The nativism that is embedded in many other countries has never really taken hold in America, because we are a nation founded by *outsiders* who became *insiders*.

3. America is the land of everything.

Dinesh D'Souza, a prominent scholar and author who grew up in Mumbai, India, paints a colorful picture of America as an amazing land of plenty. Drawing from his own experience, he writes, "The newcomer who sees America for the first time typically experiences emotions that alternate between wonder and delight. Here is a country where everything works: The roads are clean and paper-smooth; the highway signs are clear and accurate; the public toilets function properly; when you pick up the telephone, you get a dial tone; you can even buy things from the store and then take them back. For the Third World visitor, the American supermarket is a thing to behold: endless aisles of every imaginable product, 50 different types of cereal, and multiple flavors of ice cream."

Granted, these might seem like superficial characteristics—albeit those most of us take for granted. But the reason America is a land of plenty is because we have always refused to settle for less. Lacking a history of thousands of years, we decided to put our stamp on modernity. Our national mentality says if we can think it, we can make it happen. This attitude is the source of our irrepressible inventiveness, especially in technology. Google, iPhones, Amazon, Facebook, and eBay are all American creations, but so were the telephone, the airplane, credit cards, and ATMs.

Our inventiveness has a global canvas, rich with the infusion of every culture in the world. Any street or strip mall in America might contain several different ethnic restaurants. Our choice is to enjoy, borrow, and adopt from others.

4. America wants to win and is not defeated by setbacks.

America loves a comeback story, and there have been many in our history. As I've pointed out, this experiment has not always gone off without a hitch. But every downturn in our history has been followed by a greater upturn. We struggle, adapt, and thrive. The fact that our nation ever came into being in the first place is one of the most improbable stories in human history. How a ragtag band of citizens formed an army that defeated the powerful British and then chose to adopt a system of government that had never been tried is truly remarkable. The overwhelming challenges of the Civil War, the Great Depression, and the attack on Pearl Harbor, to name a few upheavals, would have brought a weaker country to its knees. But we stand today, stronger and more prosperous than ever, resilient in the face of all our problems.

We're proud of our victories, and we keep reaching higher. When I began my term at the Harvard University Asia Center as a senior research fellow on energy efficiency, I was impressed by the way institutions within the United States had taken up the challenge to tackle the massive energy problems on behalf of the world. We also decided that we were going to solve our own energy crisis, and we're making headway. Current estimates suggest that America could be energy independent by 2020—a huge technological leap that promises to make us more efficient and secure while creating a new era of manufacturing jobs. Those who worry that our manufacturing sector is dying need only look ahead to this bright prospect.

A report by the Brookings Institution summarizes this American quality of resilience: "Success in the past does not guarantee success in the future. But one thing does seem clear from the historical evidence: the American system, for all its often stultifying qualities, has also shown a greater capacity to adapt and recover from difficulties than many other nations, including its geopolitical competitors. This undoubtedly has something to do with the relative freedom of American society, which rewards innovators, often outside the existing power structure, for producing new ways of doing things; and with the relatively open political system of America, which allows movements to gain steam and to influence the behavior of the political establishment."

5. America is the economic engine for the world.

Although the United States is less than 240 years old, we are arguably the world's sole superpower and have been for some time. Our gross domestic product is $15.56 trillion, and we account for 30 percent of the world's consumer purchasing power. On average, Americans have the highest level of annual personal income of any place on the globe—at more than $50,000. The sheer power of America's economic engine is evident to anyone who has ever visited the Stock Exchange in New York City, as I have done.

Underlying this big picture is a patchwork of thousands of companies, large and small, that fuel our economic strength. The principle of meritocracy ensures that our businesses have the opportunity to succeed.

Capitalism and the free market are part of a dynamic system that rewards hard work and fresh ideas at every turn. It doesn't matter where the ideas come from, as long as they're good. For example, I don't know a country in the world that so wholeheartedly supports immigrant success. There is even a Facebook page called "America runs on immigrants."

The wonderful thing about America's economic dominance is that it is founded on a set of values that include responsibility to the community. In describing the enormous success of Starbucks, for example, its CEO, Howard Schultz, is quick to credit the company's ideology of social responsibility, saying, "The value of your company is driven by your company's values." This mentality is pervasive in businesses across the country, and I am proud to say that these values have been essential elements in the success of my own companies.

Along with this idea, a compelling aspect of our prosperity is American generosity. In 2012, while still recovering from a severe financial downturn, American individuals and corporations donated $316 billion to charity—an increase of 3.5 percent over the previous year. More impressive still, nearly 100 billionaires, led by Warren Buffett and Bill Gates, pledged to give most of their wealth to philanthropic causes. This unprecedented commitment says a lot about the American spirit. We appreciate wealth and are proud of our prosperity, but we don't hoard our riches. We share and give back and use them to create more opportunity.

6. America believes in the pursuit of happiness.

The pursuit of happiness is deemed an inalienable right in the Declaration of Independence. It is an amazingly bold choice. Nobel laureate V. S. Naipaul said it well when he said, "It implies a certain kind of society, a certain kind of awakened spirit." We talk a lot in this country about striving and working hard, but we are not talking about a long, soulless slog to success. Hard work and striving always exist in the context of seeking that inalienable right, the pursuit of happiness. Perhaps it means different things to different people, but the very fact that we cherish it sets us apart from every other country in the world.

I understand the pursuit of happiness as a permission to dream beyond the confines of your situation, no matter how lowly. Why do we struggle, why do we work, why do we study? We do all these things to achieve that which will bring fulfillment, satisfaction, inspiration. The first time I walked onto the floor of a factory I had built, my eyes filled with tears. I had achieved the happiness I had been pursuing. I've had many such experiences in my very fortunate life.

In 2013, *Time* magazine devoted a cover story to the pursuit of happiness. Author Jeffrey Kluger described it this way: "No American simply inherits happiness by dint of genes or birthplace or a brain set to sunny. Happiness, for a culture, is more like a vital sign, the temperature and heart rate of a nation. Like all vital signs, it can fluctuate. But like all vital signs, it has a set point, a level to which it strives to return. America's happiness set point has long been high and healthy—a simple gift of biology, history and environment maybe but a gift all the same. In our own loud and messy way, we've always worked to make the most of it, and we probably always will."

The pursuit of happiness gives us the freedom to dream, and dream we do. I personally believe that this is the core of what we mean by American exceptionalism. We are exceptional because we were the first new nation in centuries and we chose to build on a foundation of life, liberty, and the pursuit of happiness.

Linda Chavez, a prominent Hispanic politician and public servant, who is an advocate of open immigration, has said, "One of the chief characteristics that makes America exceptional is that we have been able to forge a common national identity among one of the most heterogeneous populations on the globe. While our political and civil institutions are grounded firmly in our Anglo-Protestant roots, we've managed within a generation or two to turn everyone from German farmers to Chinese laborers to Jewish peasants into Americans."

THE AMERICAN GIFTS OF mobility, diversity, ingenuity, generosity, productivity, liberty, and happiness are like beacons that point the way to an even better future. As a young country, our renaissance is still ahead of us.

For those who fear what the next decades will bring and wonder how they can survive the various challenges that lie ahead, I can offer volumes of advice about making it in America. But let's face it. The journey to success starts with believing, and that means cultivating a spirit of optimism. When there is doubt, let us imagine ourselves huddled with a small group of citizen legislators on a cold night in Philadelphia long ago, having to choose beyond all power of proof what was right for a new nation. Let us imagine ourselves crossing the ocean in the hull of a ship, never to return home or family because we were following a beckoning star. Let us imagine all the moments when Americans from every walk of life chose to overcome the paralysis of fear or inertia and moved ahead into the unknown. Let us remember that by striving for the principles of America, we all become guardians of that legacy. That is our exceptional story. And every one of us is part of it.

APPENDIX A
NOTES

CHAPTER 1:
THE AMERICAN DREAM:
DEAD OR ALIVE?

____ *In poll after poll*: When people are asked about the state of the American Dream, economic fears make them pessimistic. For example, a 2013 *Washington Post*–Miller Center poll shows that almost two-thirds of Americans worry about covering their basic expenses. Xavier University found that only 23 percent of survey respondents believed it would be easier for the next generation to achieve the American Dream. In June 2012 a Newport Beach market research firm reported that when asked whether they agreed with the statement that the American Dream is alive and well, 53.3 percent of those responding said no. In addition, 56.4 percent said yes when asked whether China will surpass the American way of life in our lifetime. A September 2013 *Washington Post*–Miller Center Poll found that a majority of people surveyed (61 percent) believed their children will have a better life than they have—which is a basic precept of the American Dream.

____ *In one recent survey*: A 2012 poll of college graduates by Couponcodes4u.com showed that 63 percent believed the American Dream is dead. A national study by the John J. Heldrich Center for Workforce Development at Rutgers University found that a large percentage of college graduates lack a secure career path with a full-time job and benefits. "Students who graduated during the past several years are facing historic obstacles in achieving the foundations of the American dream and express low expectations for their future prosperity," said Carl Van Horn, professor and director of the Heldrich Center and a coauthor of the study. "The resilience of this year's and recent college graduates are being tested as they struggle with student debt, a slow job market that offers few toe-holds in their chosen careers, and nagging fears about a lack of preparation for global labor market competition."

____ *A CBS News poll*: The poll conducted in March 2013 measured the level of anger at Washington. "Angry" is a much stronger word than the typical polling term "dissatisfied." The anger with Washington cut across party lines. After the government shutdown in October 2013, the number soared to 43 percent, an all-time high. www.cbsnews.com.

____ *Gallup reports*: The poll, "150 Adults Worldwide Would Migrate to the U.S.," was conducted on April 20, 2012. The potential migrants are most likely to be Chinese, Nigerian, and Indian. www.gallup.com.

____ *According to Forbes*: "40% of the Largest U.S. Companies Founded by Immigrants or Their Children." April 25, 2013. www.forbes.com.

____ *David Ho*: "David Ho—The Man Who Could Beat AIDS," by Alice Park. *Time* magazine, January 25, 2010. www.time.com.

____ *Sergey Brin*: "The Story of Sergey Brin," by Michael Malseed. *Moment* magazine, February–March 2007. www.momentmag.com.

___ *The SBA reports*: "Immigrant Entrepreneurs and Small Business Owners and Their Access to Capital," by Robert W. Farlie, Ph.D. For the SBA, May 2012. www.sba.gov.

___ *According to Partnership for a New American Economy*: "American Made 2.0—How Immigrant Entrepreneurs Continue to Contribute to the U.S. Economy," by Stuart Anderson. National Foundation for American Policy and the National Venture Capital Association. www.nvca.org. The SBA Office of Advocacy also published a report, "Estimating the Contribution of Immigrant Business Owners to the U.S. Economy," by Robert W. Fairlie, Ph.D., which used data from the Census Bureau, the Current Population Survey, and the Characteristics of Business Owners Survey to conclude that immigrant business owners make a significant contribution to business income in the United States, generating $67 billion of $577 billion total. This success is particularly notable in states with the largest immigrant populations, including New York, New Jersey, California, Texas, and Florida.

___ *According to the Immigrant Policy Center*: "Strength in Diversity: The Economic and Political Power of Immigrants, Latinos, and Asians." June 2013. The Immigration Policy Center is the research and policy arm of the American Immigration Council. www.immigrantpolicy.org.

CHAPTER 2:
THE ENDURING POWER
OF THE IMMIGRANT JOURNEY

____ *Among the Founding Fathers*: "Founding Fathers Supported Immigration," by David Bier, policy analyst at the Competitive Enterprise Institute. Biers writes: "By guaranteeing a 'uniform rule of naturalization,' the Constitution presupposes an immigrant nation. In the original conception, the Constitution protected a society of immigrants and citizens living side-by-side. While reserving the right to vote and hold office for citizens, the document, protects the rights of 'life, liberty, and property' for 'any person,' not just any citizen . . .The Founders repeatedly emphasized the benefits to the immigrants themselves. In *Common Sense*, [Thomas] Paine upheld 'this new world' as 'the asylum for the persecuted lovers of civil and religious liberty.' Jefferson argued for 'a right which nature has given to all men, of departing from the country in which chance, not choice, has placed them.' Madison defended immigration on the grounds that it is 'always from places where living is more difficult to places where it is less difficult,' so 'the happiness of the emigrant is promoted by the change.'" Huffington Post, September 20, 2012. www.huffingtonpost.com.

____ *The California Gold Rush*: *The Age of Gold—The California Gold Rush and the New American Dream*, by H.W. Brands. Anchor Books, 2008.

____ *In 1882: The Road to Chinese Exclusion—The Denver Riot, 1880 Election, and the Rise of the West*, by Liping Zhu. University Press of Kansas, 2013; *Closing the Gate—Race, Politics, and the Chinese Exclusion Act*, by Andrew Gyory. University of North Carolina Press, 1998.

___ *The Taiwanese didn't start: The Taiwanese Americans*, by Franklin Ng. Greenwood Reference, 1998. Among the notable Taiwanese Americans cited in the book are Elaine Cho, former president of the United Way, who also served in a number of high-profile business and political positions, such as director of the Peace Corps; Paul Chu, a physicist whose groundbreaking research in superconductivity is widely heralded; David Ho, the medial researcher cited in chapter 1; Yuan-Tse Lee, a chemist who studied the reaction dynamics of alkali atoms; and Chang Lien-Tien, an educator who became vice chancellor of research for the University of California, Berkeley.

___ *According to a 2012 Pew Research Report*: "Meet the New Immigrants: Asians Overtake Hispanics." The report states: "A century ago, most Asian Americans were low-skilled, low-wage laborers crowded into ethnic enclaves and targets of official discrimination. Today they are the most likely of any major racial or ethnic group in America to live in mixed neighborhoods and to marry across racial lines. When newly minted medical school graduate Priscilla Chan married Facebook founder Mark Zuckerberg last month, she joined the 37% of all recent Asian-American brides who wed a non-Asian groom . . .These milestones of economic success and social assimilation have come to a group that is still majority immigrant. Nearly three-quarters (74%) of Asian-American adults were born abroad." The report goes on to note, "Asians are the highest-earning and best-educated racial group in the country. Among Asians 25 or older, 49 percent hold a college degree, compared with 28 percent of all people in that age range in the United States. Median annual household income among Asians is $66,000 versus $49,800 among the general population." Pew Research Social and Demographic Trends. www.pewsocialtrends.org.

___ *I share the view*: "America's Real Dream Team," by Thomas L. Friedman. *The New York Times*, March 20, 2010. www.newyorktimes.com.

____ *That Used to Be Us: How America Fell behind the World It Invented and How We Can Come Back*, by Thomas L. Friedman and Michael Mandelbaum. Farrar, Strauss and Giroux, 2011.

____ *Research by UCLA*: "Comprehensive Immigration Reform Would Boost U.S. Economy," by UCLA Professor Raoul Hinojosa-Ojeda. Immigration Policy Center, January 2010. www.immigrationpolicy.org.

____ *Research by Notre Dame*: "The Economic Benefits of Passing the DREAM Act," by Juan Carlos Guzman and Raul C. Jara. Center for American Progress, September 30, 2012. www.americanprogress.org.

CHAPTER 3: CAN ANYONE STILL MAKE IT IN AMERICA?

____ *SBA Guaranty Loan*: U.S. Small Business Administration Loans. www.sba.gov/loanprograms. The SBA is a treasure trove of information and support, whether for business education, loan procurement, receiving government contracts, or networking within the business community. The website (www.sba.gov) includes an online learning center. This agency is particularly sensitive to immigrant small business development, having produced many research papers demonstrating the importance of immigrants to the small business economy.

CHAPTER 4:
INDIVIDUALS IN SMALL BUSINESS:
AMERICA'S BACKBONE AND HOPE

___ *Every year SBA hosts*: During National Small Business Week, the SBA announces the winner of its annual competition for Small Business Persons of the Year. www.sba.gov/nsbw/2013-award-winners.

___ *In February 2013, JPMorgan Chase*: 2013 Chase Business Leaders Outlook—Small Business. www.chase.com.

___ *A breakthrough came*: The DOD Mentor-Protégé Program was developed in 1991. It gives assistance to small disadvantaged businesses. Helping them to expand the overall base of their marketplace participation has produced more jobs and increased national income. The program assists small businesses in successfully competing for prime contract and subcontract awards by partnering with large companies under individual project-based agreements. Traditionally, these partnerships have delivered a variety of products and services specialized in environmental remediation, engineering services, information technology, manufacturing, telecommunications, and health care. Recently, new mentor-protégé agreements have focused on corrosion engineering, information assurance, robotics, and circuit board and metal component manufacturing. Information about the DOD's Mentor-Protégé Program is available at the U.S. Department of Defense, Office of Small Business Programs. www.acq.osd.mil/osbp/sb/programs/mpp/.

___ *Senate committee remarks*: Committee on Small Business and Entrepreneurship, U.S. Senate, One Hundred and Tenth Congress First Session, July 18, 2007.

___ *Women-owned businesses*: Women-Owned Small Business Contracting Assistance. www.sba.gov/content/contracting-opportunities-women-owned-small-businesses.

___ *The Scorecard Program*: Small Business Procurement Scorecards. www.sba.gov/content/small-business-procurement-scorecards-0. Every two years, the SBA works with each agency to set its prime and subcontracting goals, and grades are based on the agreed-upon goals. Each federal agency has a different small business contracting goal, negotiated biannually in consultation with SBA. SBA ensures that the sum total of all of the goals exceeds the 23 percent target established by law. Each agency's overall grade will show an A+ for agencies that meet or exceed 120 percent of their goals, an A for those between 100 and 119 percent, a B for 90 to 99 percent, a C for 80 to 89 percent, a D for 70 to 79 percent, and an F for less than 70 percent.

___ *In 2013 AARP reported*: "AARP Survey—Many Older Workers Start Their Own Businesses, Thrive," by Dan Well. Well writes: "Apparently the businesses formed by older workers are performing well. Almost three-quarters of older self-employed workers surveyed by AARP said their businesses were profitable in 2011 . . . Meanwhile, workers aged 65 or older are more productive and reliable than their younger cohorts are, according to a study from the Max Planck Institute for Human Development in Berlin published in the journal *Psychological Science*. 'Analyses indicate that the older adults' higher consistency is due to learned strategies to solve the task, a constantly high motivation level, as well as a balanced daily routine and stable mood,' said Dr. Florian Schmiedek of the Institute." MoneyNews, August 9, 2013. www.moneynews.com.

___ *According to the Fiscal Policy Institute*: "What Kind of Businesses Do Immigrants Own? Detail by Country of Birth." Fiscal Policy Institute, June 2012. www.fiscalpolicy.org.

___ *According to a project*: "The State of American Small Business," by Martin Neil Baily. Brookings Institution, February 1, 2012. www.brookings.edu.

___ *The SBA has a number of training programs*: Small Business Learning Center. www.sba.gov/tools/sba-learning-center. On September 27, 2010, President Obama signed into law the Small Business Jobs Act, the most significant piece of small business legislation in more than a decade. The new law is providing critical resources to help small businesses continue to drive economic recovery and create jobs. The new law extended the successful SBA-enhanced loan provisions while offering billions more in lending support, tax cuts, and other opportunities for entrepreneurs and small business owners. Among the benefits were enhanced loan provisions—more than $12 billion in lending support; higher loan limits; an expansion of the number of small businesses eligible; a temporary real estate refinancing provision; special benefits for businesses selling cars, RVs, and boats; and more equitable federal contract opportunities. The Emerging Leaders Initiative cited in the text is a great example of SBA support. This training is for established business owners and is not for start-ups or people who are thinking about starting a business. Qualifying businesses must have annual revenues of at least $300,000, have been in business for at least three years, and have at least one employee other than self.

CHAPTER 5:
PASSING THE BATON OF THE DREAM:
EDUCATION AS THE CONDUIT

____ *The educational work ethic*: The Immigrant Advantage: What We Can Learn from Newcomers to America about Health, Happiness, and Hope, by Claudia Kolker. Free Press, 2011. In her book, Kolker cites many "good habits" immigrants bring with them that contribute to success. These habits, she writes, "are not rocket science. They're based on common sense, the outcomes intuitive . . . These traits have always characterized immigrants. First-generation Americans have been more likely to be self-employed than their native-born counterparts, at least since 1880. And they're defined by their work ethic. As political scientist Francis Fukuyama points out, '[Who are] the true bearers of Anglo-Protestant values . . . who in today's world works hard? Certainly not contemporary Europeans with their six-week vacations. The real Protestants are those Korean grocery store owners, or Indian entrepreneurs, or Taiwanese engineers, or Russian cab drivers working two or three jobs in America's free and relatively unregulated labor market.'"

____ *The Georgetown University Center*: "Hard Times: College Majors, Unemployment and Earnings—Not All College Degrees Are Created Equal," by Anthony P. Carnevale, Ban Cheah, and Jeff Strohl. www.georgetown.edu.

____ *Richard Murnane*: "Assessing 21st Century Skills—Summary of a Workshop." National Academy Press, 2011.

____ *A national survey*: "Can I Get a Little Advice Here? How an Overstretched High School Guidance System Is Undermining Students' College Aspirations." A Public Agenda Report for the Bill and Melinda Gates Foundation. www.publicagenda.org.

____ *One such program*: Connecting Activities—Massachusetts School-to-Career. www.doe.mass.edu/connect/.

____ *Another impressive initiative*: "Common Goals, Unique Strength—Education and Business Partnerships." www.aasa.org.

____ *In 2002 Joel Szabat*: International Leadership Foundation. The mission of the ILF is defined as follows: to promote the civic awareness, public service, and economic effectiveness of the Asian Pacific American community and develop young leaders in the United States and other Pacific Rim countries in the fields of public service, entrepreneurship, and the international arena through a network of business and community leaders since 2000. ILF has provided scholarships, educational seminars, and leadership training for more than 1,200 college students from across the country and placed them in structured internships in government agencies. The ILF also launched an International Exchange Program in 2008, forming a U.S. Political and Business Delegation to visit Asia for the purpose of promoting leadership development and international relations in Asia and other Pacific Rim countries. With this goal in mind, ILF has successfully formed strategic alliances with international organizations that share its mission to enhance political, economic, educational, and cultural exchange programs for the mutual benefit of these countries. www.ileader.org.

____ *College Measure analyzed data*: "Two-Year Technical Degree Grads in Texas Have Higher First-Year Median Earnings than Bachelor Grads." The report pointed to two examples, Texas and Arkansas. In Texas, workers with associate's degrees in fields such as technology and health care earned a median annual salary of $50,827 in their first year after graduation, which was an average of $11,000 more than those with bachelor's degrees. In Arkansas, aircraft technicians with an occupational certificate earned, on average, more than $40,000 in the first year on the job, compared to four-year graduates with degrees in psychology who earned about $26,000. May 7, 2013. www.collegemeasures.org.

____ "Is the Four-Year, Liberal Arts Education Model Dead?" by Rob Reuteman, CNBC Business News, March 7, 2011. In his provocative piece, Reuteman writes, "A Pew Research Center survey of 220,000 incoming freshman for the 2009–2010 academic year found that 56.5 percent said it was 'very important' to pick a college whose graduates found good jobs. 'Skeptics now treat the study of liberal arts and humanities as luxuries that are not especially germane to preparing students to compete with peers from other nations in a global economy rocked by recession,' Undersecretary of Education Martha J. Kanter said in a 2010 speech. 'The implication of all this is that liberal arts colleges provide a boutique, if charmingly antiquated, education for the 21st century.'"

CHAPTER 6:
HOW AMERICA IS STILL
THE INNOVATION NATION

____ *In his book*: Who Says Elephants Can't Dance? Leading a Great Enterprise *through Dramatic Change*, by Louis V. Gerstner, Jr. HarperBusiness, 2002.

____ *A few years ago*: Innovation Nation: How America Is Losing Its *Innovation Edge, Why It Matters, and What We Can Do to Get It Back*, by John Kao. Free Press, 2007.

____ "The United States Is Quietly Losing Its Innovation Edge to China," by Yanzhong Huang. Council on Foreign Relations/Asia Unbound, October 22, 2013. blogs.cfr.org.

____ *Writing in Forbes*: "Danger: America Is Losing Its Edge in Innovation." *Forbes* magazine, January 20, 2011. www.forbes.com.

____ *ActiGraph has become*: The mission of ActiGraph is to provide its clients with highly accurate, innovative, and cost-effective objective monitoring solutions to help them achieve their research and clinical data collection, analysis, and management objectives. ActiGraph's mission is to improve world health by providing the most accurate and scientifically validated activity- and sleep-monitoring hardware and software solutions to leading research, pharmaceutical, healthcare, and wellness organizations. ActiGraph is committed to innovation, accuracy, and first-class customer service. www.actigraph.com

____ *I founded*: Ecotech Global Solutions is the primary source in China for those manufacturers who seek to increase energy efficiency, reduce costs, and demonstrate environmental stewardship. It is the first company with the credentials to undertake energy efficiency projects in China through building partnerships in China and the United States to promote research, education, product certification, technology development, and deployment but, most importantly, positive action to improve efficiency, reduce costs, and reduce emissions. Ecotech is able to source and supply energy-efficient technology and equipment from Western suppliers and arrange certification for its use in China. Because of the ambitious plans of the Chinese government, this represents a huge market for Western equipment suppliers, and Ecotech can facilitate "first-mover" status through its sourcing and certification plans. www.ecotech-global.com.

___ *Year after year*: The 2013 Global Innovation 1000 Study. www.booz.com.

___ *Google*: "Google Took Its 20% Back, but Other Companies Are Making Employee Side Projects Work for Them," by Sushma Subramanian. The author notes that "this sort of thinking is no longer only about technology companies. MTV recently surveyed Millennials on their work habits, and found that 78% believe it's important to have a side project that could become a different career. And companies of all types, from investment banks to ad firms, are now known to be explicitly tolerant of side-entrepreneurship." *Fast Company*. www.fastcompany.com.

CHAPTER 7:
THE SECRET TO THE
ENTREPRENEURIAL SPIRIT

___ *Another immigrant innovator*: "Yahoo CFO Jerry Yang," by Kate Pickert. *Time* magazine, November 19, 2008. www.time.com.

___ *A particularly inspiring*: "The Personal Side of Indra Nooyi," by Nandan Nilekani. *The Economic Times*, February 7, 2007. articles.economictimes. indiatimes.com.

___ *An immigrant entrepreneur*: Foulis Peacock's website, www. immpreneur.com, issues an invitation to immigrant entrepreneurs: "Immpreneur is a website created for *imm*igrant entre*preneurs*, or 'Immpreneurs.' Our aim is to provide content that inspires and helps Immpreneurs to launch (or grow existing) businesses in the United States." The website includes success stories of people who've come to this country, often with little savings, and built thriving businesses and successful lives in the United States. These stories focus on how to use "foreignness" as an advantage, how to start a business, how to raise financing, how to sell and market products or services, and how to navigate American business culture. For many immigrants, franchising is the first step toward business ownership in the United States, and the site has a franchising education feature, showing where the opportunities are, what qualities franchise companies are seeking in franchisees, the pitfalls to avoid, and what it really takes to build a successful franchise business. The resources and tools section helps immigrants network with other Immpreneurs from their home countries, get business advice and funding, and determine the best places in America to run a business. These organizations offer great advice, and many offer their services at no cost.

___ *Biz2Credit*: "Helping Immigrants Build Their American Dream." www.immpreneur.com. Biz2Credit is an online small business platform that matches entrepreneurs with lenders based on their business profile and preferences in a safe and price-transparent environment. www.biz2credit.com.

___ *Hungarian Tom Szaky*: "The Incredible Story of How TerraCycle CEO Tom Szaky Became a Garbage Mogul," by Kim Bhasin. *Business Insider*, August 29, 2011. www.businessinsider.com.

___ *Chobani Yogurt*: Ernst & Young World Entrepreneurial Award. www.ey.com.

___ *Not unlike my daughters*: "The Queen of Social Media," by Lindsay Blakely. *Inc.* magazine, May 28, 2013. www.inc.com.

____ *Often the next generation*: "Lifeway Kefir CEO Julie Smolyanksy Found Greatest Strength Amid Greatest Tragedy," by Emily Bennington. *Forbes* magazine, November 14, 2011. www.forbes.com.

____ *Many organizations*: Anew America Community Corporation. www. anewamerica.org. There are currently 696 Micro Enterprise Development Organizations in the United States, supporting 221,000 businesses to the tune of about $90 million. Also of note is Accion USA, which has provided more than $119 million in more than 19,000 microloans since its inception in 1991. www.accionusa.org.

____ *Writing in Psychology Today*: "Immigrant Entrepreneurs: Why Do Foreigners Make Better Entrepreneurs?" by Adrian Furnham, Ph.D. *Psychology Today*, September 28, 2013. www.psychologytoday.com.

____ *Nassim Taleb*: "Who Are the Most Successful Immigrants in the World?" Transcript of a radio broadcast between Stephen J. Dubner and Nassim Taleb. August 29, 2013. www.freakonomics.com. Another relevant resource is Richard T. Herman's book, *Immigrant, Inc.: Why Immigrant Entrepreneurs Are Driving the New Economy (and How They Will Save the American Worker*, Wiley 2009.

____ *According to the Global Entrepreneurship Monitor*: "Tracking Success among Immigrant Entrepreneurs," by Patrick Clark. Blomberg Businessweek, June 24, 2013. www.businessweek.com.

____ *Karen Gordon Mills*: "A Nation of Immigrants and Entrepreneurs," by Karen Gordon Mills. August 7, 2013. www.sba.gov.

___ *That reality was the basis*: Blueseed: The Startup Community on a Ship. www.blueseed.com.

___ *I subscribe to the idea*: Consortium for Entrepreneurial Education. www.entre-ed.com.

CHAPTER 8:
EMBRACING THE GIFT OF DIVERSITY

___ *At Eglin*: "Economic Impact of the Military in Northwest Florida," by Scott T. Jackson. *Business Magazine of NW Florida*, December 2009; *I Came Back from Bataan*, by Robert Whitmore. Amazon Digital Services, 2012. In his book Whitmore offers a moving tribute to Jo's family and their lifesaving intervention on behalf of the prisoners of war.

___ *Recalling his personal journey*: *Immigration Wars: Forging an American Solution*, by Jeb Bush and Clint Bolick. Threshold Editions, 2013.

___ *Among those*: Edward Roberts, David Sarnoff professor of management of technology, founder and chair, Martin Trust Center for MIT Entrepreneurship. www.mitsloan.edu.

___*A research report*: "Reforming Immigration Law to Allow More Foreign Student Entrepreneurs to Launch Job-Creating Ventures in the United States," by John Norton and Malika Simmons of the UMKC Institute for Entrepreneurship and Innovation and the UMKC School of Law, for the Ewing Marion Kauffman Foundation. The Kauffman Foundation for Entrepreneurship has developed a comprehensive resource center for entrepreneurs, including immigrant entrepreneurs. Its online video series,

"America's Great Job Creators: Immigrant Entrepreneurs," offers inspiring and instructive stories. www.kauffman.org.

___ *As Shayan Zedeh*: "Bring on More Immigrant Entrepreneurs," by Shayan Zedeh. *The Wall Street Journal*, November 5, 2013.

___ *This idea supports*: "America's Real Dream Team," by Thomas L. Friedman. *The New York Times*, March 20, 2010. www.newyorktimes.com.

___ *The good news*: A survey by the Rockefeller Foundation: http://www.philanthropynewsdigest.org/news/majority-of-americans-support-diversity-new-equality-agenda-survey-finds#sthash.xNymMYYb.dpuf.

___ *As Michael Barone*: "A Nation Built for Immigrants: Will the Recent Surge of Newcomers Tear the U.S. Apart? Not If History Is Any Guide: From the Beginning, America Was Made to Unite Citizens, Even Those with Deep Differences," by Michael Barone. *The Wall Street Journal*, September 20, 2013. The article is based on Barone's book, *Shaping Our Nation: How Surges of Migration Transformed America and Its Politics*, Crown Forum, 2013.

___ *In the summer of 2013*: "Letter from Business Urges Congress to Create a 21st Century Immigration System." www.immigrationimpact.com.

___ *Even the League of Women Voters*: "Immigrants: Diversity and Inclusion," by Deborah Macmillan. www.lwv.org.

___ *The New Immigrant Survey*: www.migrationinformation.org.

___ *Another important study*: The George W. Bush Institute. www.bush-center.org/george-w-bush-institute.

___ *Karen Kaminsky*: "A Conversation on Immigration-Culture Project." July 18, 2012. www.youtube.com.

___ *Davuliri is part*: This anecdotal evidence is supported by a report from the Immigrant Learning Center. "Adult Children of Immigrant Entrepreneurs: Memories and Influence" shares the stories of 36 children of immigrants representing a wide variety of countries of origin and family businesses. Some were born in the United States, and others immigrated here in childhood. According to the report, "While their stories differ, they all have one thing in common: their immigrant entrepreneur parents and experiences growing up around the family business heavily influenced their desire to pursue an education and the American dream." Lisa Park's book, *Consuming Citizenship: Children of Asian Immigrant Entrepreneurs* (Stanford University Press, 2005), also makes this case.

___ *Test*: "Could You Pass a US Citizenship Test?" *The Christian Science Monitor*. www.csmonitor.com.

___ *The oath of citizenship*: I hereby declare, on oath, that I absolutely and entirely renounce and abjure all allegiance and fidelity to any foreign prince, potentate, state, or sovereignty of whom or which I have heretofore been a subject or citizen; that I will support and defend the Constitution and laws of the United States of America against all enemies, foreign and domestic; that I will bear true faith and allegiance to the same; that I will bear arms on behalf of the United States when required by law; that I will perform noncombatant service in the Armed Forces of the United States when required by the law; that I will perform work of national importance under civilian direction when required by the law; and that I take this obligation freely without any mental reservation or purpose of evasion; so help me God.

CHAPTER 9:
BELIEVING IN AMERICA . . .
WHO ARE THE GUARDIANS?

____ *As a young man*: "What Happened to Taiwan's Little League Champs?" by Samuel Chi. *The Diplomat*, August 15, 2013.

____ *America the Beautiful: Rediscovering What Made This Nation Great*, by Ben Carson, M.D. Zondervan, 2012.

____ *America's welcoming nature*: "Why the U.S. Is So Good at Turning Immigrants into Americans," by Jason DeParle. *The Atlantic*, October 23, 2013; "Immigration Assimilation and the Measure of an American," by Stephanie Hanes. *The Christian Science Monitor*, July 7, 2013.

____ *As the noted scholar*: "The Challenge for European Identity," by Francis Fukiyama. *The Global Journal*, January 11, 2012.

____ *A sense of identity*: "America, the Great Experiment," by Peter and Helen Evans. *Renew America*, June 22, 2003.

____ *Colin Powell writes movingly of the America he knows and loves*: "As I traveled the world as secretary of state, I encountered anti-American sentiment. But I also encountered an underlying respect and affection for America. People still want to come here. Refugees who have no home at all know that America is their land of dreams. Even with added scrutiny, people line up at our embassies to apply to come here. "You see, I believe that the America of 2005 is the same America that brought Maud Ariel McKoy and Luther Powell to these shores, and so many millions of others. An America that each day gives new immigrants the same gift that my parents received. An America that lives by a Constitution that inspires freedom and democracy around the world. An America with a big, open, charitable heart that reaches out to people in need around the world. An America that sometimes seems confused and is always noisy. That noise has a name, it's called democracy and we use it to work through our confusion. An America that is still the beacon of light to the darkest corner of the world."

___ *Dinesh D'Souza*: "What's Great about America," by Dinesh D'Souza. The Heritage Foundation, February 23, 2006.

___ *A report by Brookings*: "Not Fade Away—Against the Myth of American Decline," by Robert Kagan. The Brookings Institution, January 17, 2012.

___ *Along with this idea*: "American Generosity Second to None," by Vincenzina Santoro. Mercatornet.com, August 19, 2013. The article cites research by the Center on Philanthropy at Indiana University, in collaboration with the Giving USA Foundation, which published a survey entitled "Giving USA," providing data on private donations to charitable and nonprofit organizations in the United States, including to those that primarily operate internationally. The latest edition indicated that in 2012 American individuals and corporations donated $316 billion to charity, representing 2 percent of gross domestic product. This was an increase of 3.5 percent over the previous year. Despite a weak economy, relatively high unemployment, and near stagnant wages, individuals accounted for more than 72 percent, or $229 billion, of all donations, a 3.9 percent gain from the year before that was higher than the overall average. http://www.merca-tornet.com/articles/view/american_generosity_second_to_none#sthash.MjE9heSc.dpufhttp://www.mercatornet.com/articles/view/american_gen-erosity_second_to_none#sthash.MjE9heSc.dpuf.

___ *In 2013 Time* magazine: "The Pursuit of Happiness," by Jeffrey Kruger. *Time* magazine, July 8, 2013.

___ *Nobel Laureate*: Naipaul made this statement at a lecture at the Manhattan Institute in 1990, further saying, "This idea of the pursuit of happiness is at the heart of the attractiveness of the civilization to so many outside it or on its periphery. I find it marvelous to contemplate to what an extent, after two centuries, and after the terrible history of the earlier part of this century, the idea has come to a kind of fruition. It is an elastic idea; it fits all men. It implies a certain kind of society, a certain kind of awakened spirit. I don't imagine my father's Hindu parents would have been able to understand the idea. So much is contained in it: the idea of the individual, responsibility, choice, the life of the intellect, the idea of vocation and perfectibility and achievement. It is an immense human idea. It cannot be reduced to a fixed system. It cannot generate fanaticism. But it is known to exist, and because of that, other more rigid systems in the end blow away."

ACKNOWLEDGMENTS

I have always been blessed by the people around me. None of us achieves success on our own. I would not be where I am today without the great outpouring of love and support I have received at every step of my journey.

First and foremost, there is Maggie, who has made my life possible. She is the source of my strength and my happiness. Our three remarkable children, Jessica, John, and Jennifer, have filled our lives with joy, and as adults they have delighted us with their creativity and vision. I am the luckiest husband and father in the world!

I am forever indebted to the love and support of my mother, my brother Peter, my late brother John, and my sister Angela.

This book could not have happened without a community of support. I am grateful to Jerry Jenkins and Leah Nicholson for their guidance and enthusiasm. They have helped me negotiate the unfamiliar world of publishing and given me access to talented professionals. Catherine Whitney heard my voice and message and transformed my words and ideas into prose that reflects my deep passion about America. Mike Greece has been a constant presence, helping me figure out the best way to present my book. His creativity and range of knowledge have been invaluable.

Back in the beginning, as a young student new to this country, I was lifted up by David and Mary Miller, who took me on and showed me the way. Their love and support lasted throughout my life. Sadly, David passed away last year. I want this book to be a tribute to him, my first mentor and friend in America.

Keith Biggs and Jeff Arnett, who head my two companies, are more than partners. They have become like brothers to me. I am so grateful to have them in my life. I also am appreciative of the support and contribution of Kim Perez, Maria Arnett, George Sims, and Joe Cothron.

Over the years, many people have stepped up to help me, advise me, and partner with me. They are all part of my success, and I owe them a debt of gratitude, especially John Brinkley, Stan Davis, Don Gaetz, Joe Scarborough, Willie Gonzalez, Herschel Jackson, Bill Kirk, Cliff Long, Hervis Ward, Bob Patterson, Bob Chedister, Ralph Frangioni, Tony Deluca, Joe McLure, David Goetsch, Larry Sassano, Jim Breitenfeld, Chiling Tong, Joel Szabat, Bob Keller, Jack Lippert, Ming Lam, Johnny Tsoi, Sherry Campbell, Helen Hsiang, Ming Chang, Jon Mills, Arthur Kleinman, Holly Angell, Maggie Zone, Bill Overhold, Elizabeth Liao, Bill Stowers, Jerry Denniels, Hank Princeville, Frank Smith, Sam Calloway, Angela Cheng, Michael Cheng, Jonathan Lin, Glenn Scharf, Myra Williams, Mal McGree, and Reneé de la Cruz.

ABOUT THE AUTHOR

DR. PAUL HSU

An American patriot, businessman, industrial engineer, and lifelong entrepreneur, Dr. Paul Hsu is the chairman of Hsu Enterprise Group LLC, a global environmental engineering and renewable energy company specializing in energy-efficient technologies such as clean coal production.

Born in Taiwan, Paul came to the United States as a first-generation immigrant in 1976. His first company, Manufacturing Technology Inc. (MTI), was founded in 1984 and provided avionics and electronics solutions for the Department of Defense. After MTI, Paul founded three more successful companies beginning with Total Parts Plus Inc., an internet-based data management and content provider; Actigraph LLC, an electronic medical device manufacturer; and his current company, HSU Enterprise Group LLC.

In 2007, Paul was appointed associate administrator of the Office of Government Contractive and Business Development by President Bush and in 2010 member of the National Minority Business Advisory Board by President Obama. Paul also is a senior research fellow in energy efficiency at Harvard University Asia Center.

Since coming to the United States, Paul has been active in public service at all levels, including the U.S. President's Export Council, the U.S. SBA National Advisory Board, U.S. SBA's Regulatory Enforcement

Fairness Board, the USAF Chief of Staff Civic Leadership Advisory Group, Florida's Sustainable Emerald Coast Committee, Enterprise Florida Inc., the Okaloosa-Walton College Foundation, the Emerald Coast Science Center, the University of West Florida Foundation, and the Economic Development Council Okaloosa County, Florida Board. Paul has worked closely with international organizations such as the China Association of Resource Comprehensive Utilization (CARCU), the China Quality Certification Center (CQC), and the U.S.-China Cooperation on Energy and Climate Change.

His awards include the SBA's National Small Business Prime Contractor of the Year, SBA's Small Business Person of the Year, the State of Florida Governor's Award of Excellence, the Department of Defense (DOD) "Quality Vendor," and the Nunn-Perry Award. In June 2001, Paul was the recipient of the Ernst & Young Entrepreneur of the Year Award for the state of Florida in the technology/communications category. In 2003, Paul was inducted into the SBA's Hall of Fame, and in 2004, he received the Corporate Stewardship Award from the U.S. Chamber of Commerce.

Additionally, Paul and his family have invested significant time and resources in community building across America. In 2006, he served as the national chairman of the International Leadership Foundation, an organization that brings young leaders from other countries to Washington, D.C., for summer internships. In 2002, he established the Dr. Paul and Majes-Maggie Hsu Engineering Scholarship for outstanding engineering students.

He and his wife, Maggie, live in Florida. They have three children.